ICSC
United States Design and Development Awards

2009 Finalists

P9-DOC-677

The ICSC U.S. Design and Development Awards are designed to honor and recognize the premier design and development trends of retail projects and retail store design within the U.S. These awards only enhance and compliment the Design and Development Award programs currently offered by ICSC and will bring information and insight to the entire industry on what it takes to achieve the highest level of recognition in design and development within the U.S.

Winners of ICSC's U.S. Design and Development Awards program, along with winners from other regional design and development programs, will automatically be entered into the ICSC's Global Design and Development Awards competition, the Best-of-the-Best, and eligible to be named "The Shopping Center of the Year" or the "Best Sustainability Project". ICSC's Best-of-the-Best Awards honor and recognize the most outstanding examples of shopping center design and development, sustainability, marketing, and community service worldwide. The winners of the Best-of-the-Best Awards are announced during RECon, ICSC's annual convention in Las Vegas, Nevada, May 2010.

Winning Shopping Center Designs

Renovation or Expansion of
an Existing Project
Retail Projects less than
150,000 sq. ft. of total retail space

Lincoln & Rose Venice, California

Owner/Development/Management/ Leasing Company: Combined Properties Incorporated
Design/Production/Executive Architect: Studio One Eleven
Graphic Designer: Newsom Design
Lighting Designer: USA Architectural Lighting
Landscape Architect: EPT Design
General Contractor: A.J. Padelford & Son Inc.

Total Retail Space: 75,327 sq. ft.
Number of Stores: 3

Lincoln & Rose is the revitalization of an existing 75,000 square foot retail center along Lincoln Boulevard in Venice, California. Originally built in the 1960s, the shopping center had become blighted: it suffered from awkward additions, an influx of low-rent tenants, crime, and general disrepair. The primary objective of the project was to transform the site into a community gathering place and attract tenants that would be beneficial to the area. The project modifies the interior spaces to accommodate a large-scale supermarket anchor, increases the width of sidewalks to encourage pedestrian activity, establishes an inviting atmosphere, and creates a distinctive and innovative building exterior that reflects the character of this unique beachside neighborhood. The redevelopment of the old shopping center included an extensive façade renovation, new exterior lighting, a new site and landscape plan, and a cohesive signage program. The contemporary building material palette features a pattern of textured and colored stucco, steel, colored glass, metal panels, clear anodized storefront, burnished concrete block, bamboo plywood, and a variety of wood siding. Demolition was minimized: the original canopy of the building was removed, but many of the new building materials were installed directly over the existing façade. Steel trellis structures with wood siding were constructed around the existing pad building at the corner of Lincoln Blvd. and Machado Dr. to conceal the sloped roof. The sidewalk design is inspired by the beach, including decorative concrete with shell and pebble aggregate. After closing hours, the exterior sales areas are secured by lowering the façade's distinctive mechanized wood and steel gates.

Renovation or Expansion of
an Existing Project
Retail Projects 150,001 sq. ft.
to 500,00 sq. ft. of total retail space

Royal Hawaiian Center Honolulu, Hawaii

Development Company: The Festival Companies
Owner: Kamehameha Schools
Design/Production/Executive Architect/Graphic Designer: Callison Architecture
Lighting Designer: Horton Lees Brogden Lighting Design
Landscape Architect: EDAW
General Contractor: Charles Pankow Builders, Ltd.
Management Company: Festival Management Corporation
Leasing Company: Festival Management Corporation

Total Retail Space: 310, 000 sq. ft.
Number of Stores: 108

The three-block center consists of three main buildings interconnected with bridges, elevators and escalators that easily move visitors throughout its four levels. To take advantage of the ample pedestrian foot traffic in the area, new pathways connect the Center to the surrounding hotels. Additionally, a performance theater and restaurants with outdoor seating areas overlooking the courtyards and Kalakaua Avenue are strategically positioned on the third and fourth levels to improve the Center's vertical circulation by drawing visitors to the upper levels. The Hawaiian-inspired design elements celebrate the local environment and allow visitors to enjoy the open-air attributes of the Center, which is nestled among palm trees and tiki torches. Several lanai decks feature vistas and views of the surrounding area. Native landscaping and the use of extended beams and trellises provide a comforting filter from the bright sunlight. The trellises, inspired by Hawaiian outrigger canoes, help soften the hard, exterior edges of the Center's existing buildings. A new foot bridge connecting the central buildings overlooks the historic Royal Grove and runs alongside a large, tropical banyan tree with suspended glowing lanterns. A dynamic mix of 110 world-class retailers, restaurants and entertainment destinations caters to both local residents and visitors. Several high-end luxury retailers occupy street-front townhouse-style stores along Kalakaua Avenue such as Hermes, Fendi, Cartier, Bulgari and Salvatore Ferragamo.

Renovation or Expansion of an Existing Project
Retail Projects more then 500,001 sq. ft. of total retail space

Bayshore Town Center Glendale, Wisconsin

Development/Management/
 Leasing Company: Steiner + Associates
Owner: Bayshore Town Center, LLC
Design Architect: Development Design Group Inc
Production/Executive Architect: Eppstein Uhen
Executive Architect: Meacham + Apel (Building N)
Graphic Designer: David Carter Design Associates
Lighting Designer: Powrtek Engineering Inc
Landscape Architect: Graef, Anhalt, Schloemer & Associates and
 David J. Frank, Landscape Contractors, Inc
General Contractor: Hunzinger Construction Co and
 Corna Kokosing Construction Company
Finance Company: HSBC

Total Retail Space: 1,020,818 sq. ft.
Number of Stores: 137

Bayshore Town Center integrates residential, retail, dining, office, a health club and two freestanding pavilions framing a central town square into the partial demolition and renovation of a preexisting indoor mall. The project is located six miles north of downtown Milwaukee. A hybrid town center and enclosed mall, Bayshore includes an eclectic blend of architectural styles, featuring a prominent two-level octagonal grand rotunda, a powerful linking element between indoor and outdoor components. The heart of the new Bayshore, the rotunda includes double-height windows and clear stories, and opens onto a valet plaza. A connecting walkway runs from the rotunda to an adjacent parking deck. The Grand Hall highlights the interior renovation, using windows, light fixtures, graphics and signage to convey the impression of a street transformed into a covered, colorfully animated retail galleria. The project features over 215,000 square feet of office and 115 loft-style residential-above-retail apartments, while 75 condominium-style residences laminate the four-level eastern parking deck and interface with adjacent neighborhoods. A diverse mix of restaurant, retail and entertainment options includes an eight-screen art-house cinema and a comedy club. Brick and stone facades and copper roofing add Milwaukee character and architectural flavor, while outward-facing retail engages the surrounding community and integrates with an existing commercial avenue.

Clackamas Town Center Portland, Oregon

Owner/Development/Management/Finance/
 Leasing Company: General Growth Properties
Design/Production/Executive Architect: DLR Group
Graphic Designer: RSM Design
Lighting Designer: Luma Lighting Design
Landscape Architect: Nevue Ngan
General Contractor: Howard S. Wright Construction Company

Total Retail Space: 1,461,220 sq. ft.
Number of Stores: 261

Clackamas Town Center has been reborn, shedding its former role as a suburban mall to become a true town center. Originally constructed in 1981, the mall in Clackamas County, Oregon, was designed to meet the car-centric suburban shopping expectations of the era. The only improvements during the past two decades included an interiors upgrade in 1994. Despite its ideal location at the confluence of an interstate, a major arterial, and a state highway, the mall was all but invisible. Its outdated design was hidden behind nondescript massive boxes and a sea of parking. By adding approximately 324,000 square feet of new retail space, the mall's character and function is dramatically improved, increasing its gross leasable area to 1,475,000 square feet. The Northwest Metropolitan design concept fuses nature's organic warmth with the industrial chic character of urban loft neighborhoods, evoking the best qualities of Portland, Clackamas County, and the greater Pacific Northwest community that the center serves. This previously inward-facing mall now reaches out to shoppers and the surrounding community; the existing sea of parking now supports a thriving regional mass transit system; the new exterior pedestrian experience connects formerly isolated shopping center areas and provides space for community events. As these improvements have elevated the mall to true shopping destination status, so have they propelled its retail success.

Innovative Design and Development of a New Project
Retail Projects less than
150,000 sq. ft. of total retail space

Court Street, San Luis Obispo San Luis Obispo, California

Development/Management Company: Copelands Properties
Owner: CP Court Street, LLC
Design Production/Executive Architect/Graphic Designer: Mark Rawson, AIA
Lighting Designer: Thoma Electric
Landscape Architect: FIRMA
General Contractor: JW Design and Construction
Finance Company: Rabobank
Leasing Company: Fandel Retail Group

Total Retail Space: 49,044 sq. ft.
Number of Stores: 11

The Court Street Project is an open air retail specialty center located in the Historic District of Downtown San Luis Obispo at the site of a former parking lot. The project is carefully crafted to be compatible with surrounding historic buildings and although constructed as one three story building, it is designed to appear as several buildings to blend with the scale and variety of the surrounding areas. Retail is located on two primary levels—the project's upper retail level fronts onto a pedestrian walkway which connects opposite corners of the project site. A grand stair and terrace connect the pedestrian walk to the street frontage at ground level and serves as an informal seating/gathering area during the weekly Thursday night farmer's markets. Another pedestrian only walk street serves the lower retail level and provides opportunities for outdoor dining and restaurant seating.

Innovative Design and Development of a New Project
Retail Projects over 500,000 sq. ft. of total retail space

Town Square Las Vegas Las Vegas, Nevada

Owner/Development/ Management Company: Turnberry Associates and Centra Properties
Design Architect/Graphic Designer: Development Design Group Inc
Materials Consultant: Mayer & Associates
Production/Executive Architect: Marnell Corrao Associates
Lighting Designer: Francis Krahe & Associates
Landscape Architect: Lifescapes International
General Contractor: Marnell Corrao Associates
Finance Company: Deutsche Bank Inc
Leasing Company: Turnberry Associates

Total Retail Space: 897,383 sq. ft.
Number of Stores: 132

A lifestyle destination that breaks the traditional town square mold, Town Square features a compelling combination of public parks, retail, office, dining and entertainment options. Located on the Vegas Strip, the project is at the heart of the action in Las Vegas. Town Square offers an array of retail options and boutique shops oriented around a central town square with fountains and courtyards. Family-friendly facilities include a children's park with a carousel, bookstores, art galleries, gourmet market and an 80,000 square foot, 18-screen second-level multiplex theater. A revolutionary concept for Las Vegas, the unique format channels vibrant Vegas energy into an innovative new neighborhood-style retail and entertainment community. Telling evidence of this new approach is the conspicuous absence of those iconic Vegas landmarks: casinos. Town Square includes over 200,000 square feet of loft office space above street-level retail and a boutique hotel is planned. A collage of different architectural styles from Old World-styled, Spanish mission-inspired pueblo-deco, to contemporary town center styling and Mediterranean influences confer an organic sensibility, conveying the impression that the town has evolved over time. Abundant green space and tree-lined, colonnaded avenues shaded with trellises and canopies soften the streetscape, enabling the city's two million residents and 40 million annual tourists to experience a fresh new approach to Las Vegas design.

Winter Garden Village at Fowler Groves Winter Garden, Florida

Development/Management/Leasing Company: The Sembler Company
Owner: Cole Capital
Design Architect/Graphic Designer: Architecture Plus International
Production/Executive Architect: Lyman Davidson Dooley
Graphic Designer: Architecture Plus International
Finance Company: Wachovia

Total Retail Space: 1,144,342 sq. ft.
Number of Stores: 87

Winter Garden Village at Fowler Groves is a 1,150,000 square foot, open-air shopping center located in the burgeoning submarket of Orange County in the Orlando area. The project boasts 150 acres of retail that is 100% built out and a 25 acre multi-family residential parcel. Since opening in October 2007, Winter Garden Village has become an integral part of the community having created over 2,200 jobs and annually generating approximately $2 million in ad valorem tax, the most of any tax paying entity in the City of Winter Garden. Winter Garden Village is divided into three sections: The Exchange, The Crossings and The Grove. The Exchange represents the largest big box retailers and sits along the 429 Expressway. The Crossings along Daniels Road, features outparcels and community-scale services while The Grove is the lifestyle retail component and is considered the heart of the shopping center with the soaring Clock Tower as its center-piece. Winter Garden Village's design borrows from a vast palette of historic architecture, creating a collection of four-sided retail storefronts meant to look like a main street built over time. At street level, lush landscaping, outdoor seating and a public art collection create a sense of place and the easily accessible connectors throughout the surface parking help make the village walk-able and safe

Innovative Design and Development
of a New Project
Mixed-Use Projects

The Americana at Brand Glendale, California

Owner/Development /Management/ Finance/Leasing Company: Caruso Affiliated
Design Architect: Elkus/Manfredi Architects
Production/Executive Architect: Harley Ellis Devereaux
Graphic Designer: Romero Thorsen Design
Lighting Designer: Visual Terrain
Landscape Architect: Lifescapes International
General Contractor: Bernards Builders

Total Retail Space: 454,000 sq. ft.
Number of Stores: 75

The Americana at Brand is ten miles north of Los Angeles in Glendale, California, home to 200,000 residents. Located in a mature downtown, The Americana at Brand replaced eight blighted city blocks next to the 1.6 million square foot Glendale Galleria and is bordered by major north/south and east/west thoroughfares connecting the site to four major freeways. This traditionally styled mixed-use development is the symbolic heart of Glendale and destination of choice for residents and visitors from 111 zip codes throughout Southern California. Designed in the tradition of great public spaces, The Americana at Brand recovers that which is lost in Southern California's car culture: the sense of community that comes from street life and fulfilling the desire to connect with the community. The open spaces are lined by shops and restaurants, animated water and light and by residents who live on the park, who step out onto terraces and balconies to enjoy it. It is interwoven into the existing context of the city, yet separate from its traffic and noise. This concept is proving to have strength through the recent downturn in the economy. Attendance is very strong and tenants are experiencing sales at or near the top in their chains. The Americana at Brand combines the best that street front retail has to offer with the marketing strength, amenities, convenient parking and secure environment that a managed private development can offer.

Bridge Street Town Centre Huntsville, Alabama

Owner/Development/Management/Leasing Company: O&S Holdings, LLC
Design Architect: TSD Design Group, Inc.
Production/Executive Architect: TSArchitects
Graphic Designer: ID8
Lighting Designer: Visual Terrain, Inc.
Landscape Architect: EDAW Inc.
General Contractor: Winter Construction and ValleyCrest Landscape Development
Finance Company: Wells Fargo Bank NA

Total Retail Space: 450,000 sq. ft.
Number of Stores: 66

Bridge Street Town Centre is a mixed-use project composed of high-end retail shops, a 14-plex upscale movie theater, a Class-A office building and an upscale hotel centered around a 10-acre man-made lake. The concept was to create a retail street reminiscent of a Mediterranean village which would be so unique and timeless that it would draw people from not only the adjacent areas immediately surrounding Huntsville, but also a destination center that would draw people from the adjacent towns. There are fourteen separate retail buildings (including the movie theater) few of which are on the same angle with each other. This was done to create the main meandering street with nooks and side streets that gives people a real sense of place. In order to achieve a sense of time-lessness the building materials were varied so that the center didn't appear to have been constructed at the same time. Some of the aesthetic issues dealt with were centered on the issues of creating an authentic/timeless project. Plaster and stone facades lend authenticity, as do varying roof heights, having dummy second floors with lights that come on behind the windows at night. The plaster colors, two-piece clay tile roof mixes and the stone mixes were all varied. The first phase of what will eventually be a 2 million square foot retail/office/residential/hotel complex opened in November 2007 with 450,000 square feet of retail and a 132,000 square foot 5-story Class-A office building and a 14-story Westin hotel/condominium use.

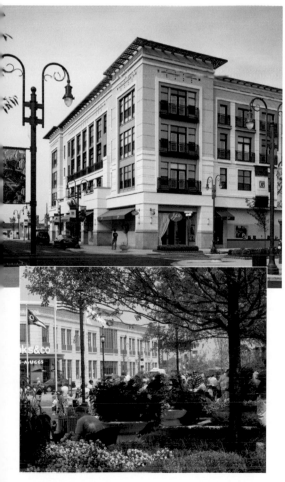

The Greene Beavercreek, Ohio

Owner/Development/Management/ Leasing Company: Steiner + Associates
Design Architect: Development Design Group Inc.
Design Architect: Torti Gallas and Partners (Building C)
Production/Executive Architect: Meacham + Apel
Graphic Designer: David Carter Design Associates
Lighting Designer: Grenald Waldron
Landscape Architect: Edge Group
General Contractor: Messer Construction
Finance Company: HSBC

Total Retail Space: 411,892 sq. ft.
Number of Stores: 77

The Greene, designed around a progressive mix of Midwestern mercantile architectural styles features regional shopping, dining and a residential district. Approximately 400,000 square feet of retail and restaurants, an 80,000 s.f. stadium-seating cinema and 150 loft-style residences overlook The Greene's fountained town square and central park. The project also features 100,000 square feet of high-tech office suites. Phase 2 includes a full-service hotel. By placing residential components in a prominent manner, The Greene achieves a level of established authenticity; a mix of shopping and living that creates the dense livable space of a town that has evolved over time. Civic anchors, rather than retail icons, evoke architectural memories of a firehouse, town hall, bank and library. These echoes of a traditional main street are positioned at key visual intersections along streets and park corners. Two large farmers market buildings, complete with restaurants and small shops, bracket the town square. The Greene's use of colors, textures and traditional brick-and-stone materials, and its canopies, colonnades and outdoor dining options infuses the project with life and vitality. The result is a mixed-use destination that enlivens the public square and encourages residents and visitors to engage, experience and explore their environment.

The Kansas City Power & Light District Kansas City, Missouri

Owner/Development/Management/Leasing/Finance Company: The Cordish Company
Design Architect: Beyer Blinder Belle
Production/Executive Architect: 360 Architecture, Booth Hansen, Rafael Architects Inc.,
 and Helix Architecture
Graphic Designer: Selbert Perkins Design
Lighting Designer: Lighting Design Alliance
Landscape Architect: Young & Dring Landscape Architects
General Contractor: JE Dunn Construction Co. and
 KC Live LLC with Jess Burts Enterprises as owner's Representation

Total Retail Space: 600,000 sq. ft.
Number of Stores: 50

Kansas City Power & Light District, Kansas City, Missouri, was developed as a part of
a public-private partnership with the City of Kansas City and the State of Missouri.
The District was the culmination of forty year City efforts that transformed an area of
urban blight into a vibrant downtown core which now attracts 8 million visitors. The
$850 million, nine city block, mixed-use district encompasses 600,000 SF of retail
entertainment, 1 million SF of office, hotels, civic and sports venues and more. Highlights
include the expanded 400,000 SF Bartle Hall Convention Center, the 18,000 seat Sprint
Center Arena, H&R Block's World Headquarters, the 4-star 213 room President Hilton
Hotel, two restored historic theaters (the Empire and the Midland), Cosentino's Market
(the City's first downtown grocery store), the new home of The Kansas City Repertory
Theater, and KC Live! a city block of open-air plaza featuring restaurants and entertainment venues surrounding a public events space. The District was masterplanned in
an environmentally sensitive manner to incorporate public space and roof top parks.

The Market Common, Myrtle Beach Myrtle Beach, South Carolina

Development/Management/Leasing Company: McCaffery Interests, Inc.
Owner: LUK-MB1, LLC; McCaffery Interests, Inc., Leucadia International Corporation
Design Production/Executive Architect: Antunovich Associates
Graphic Designer/Landscape Architect: Sasaki Associates, Inc.
General Contractor: Plant Construction, Construction Management of 8 contractors
Finance Company: Leucadia National, JP Morgan Chase City of MB

Total Retail Space: 350,000 sq. ft.
Number of Stores: 49

The Market Common, Myrtle Beach (MCMB) is a masterplanned, mixed-use development
strategically situated on 121 acres of a portion of the larger 3,790 acre former United States
Air Force Base in Myrtle Beach, South Carolina. The Air Force Base was fully operational
until 1993 when it was closed. The MCMB fulfills the vision of reopening the base to the
public for parks, schools and roadways and private investment. When fully developed,
the former Air Force Base will contain over 4,500 home sites, 3 million sf of commercial
uses, 400 acres of institutional uses and 200 acres of parks, recreational facilities and open
space. The MCMB is the new urban village for Myrtle Beach and indeed the entire Grand
Strand area. The MCMB development has been planned to be completed in 3 phases over
a 5 year period. Phase 1 contains 25 acres and has extensive frontage along Farrow Parkway.
This phase adds over 350,000 sf of retail and restaurant uses, 195 rental apartments
above the retail, over 45,000 sf of office, 1,700 surface and structured parking stalls,
and 5 acres of parks and open space—all in a mixed-use urban village format. This phase
was completed on April 3, 2008. The retail, restaurant and rental apartment uses within
Phase 1 are situated along two main pedestrian-oriented boulevards integrated with
amenities such as water features, gazebos, a children's play lot, and richly landscaped areas.

Cole Haan Factory Store Philadelphia Premium Commons
Limerick, Pennsylvania

Company: Cole Haan
Architect/Designer: Callison
General Contractor: Hirsch Construction.

Type of Merchandise: Apparel

Targeted to luxury customers, the clean, natural design enhances Cole Haan's classic products. Cole Haan's new factory store concept provides a chic, casual shopping environment. The design employs strong horizontal lines, with low sightlines and merchandising organized by style rather than size for ease of shopping. The new concept allows for a focused presentation that has elevated the Cole Haan brand among the upscale outlet retailers and streamlined its brand portfolio.

Target Atlanta Midtown at Atlantic Station
Atlanta, Georgia

Company: Target Corporation
Architect/Designer: Target Corporation
General Contractor: H. J. Russell and Company

Type of Merchandise: General Merchandise

Atlantic Station Overview: The Atlantic Station community is a national model for smart growth and sustainable real estate development. Master developed by AIG Global Real Estate and officially opened in 2005, the 138-acre community is an environmental redevelopment and reclamation of the former Atlantic Steel Mill. Located at the nexus of Interstates 75 and 85 in Midtown Atlanta, Atlantic Station is ultimately projected to include 12 million square feet of retail, office, residential and hotel space as well as 11 acres of public parks. Providing homes for 10,000 people, employment opportunities for 30,000 and shopping and entertainment options for millions more, this 24-hour neighborhood buzzes as one of the premier live/work/play communities in the United States. Target Atlanta Midtown at Atlantic Station is a unique Target Store in its urban siting, program variation, architectural expression and aspiration, building materiality and landscape design. Target Corporation operates over 2,000 General Merchandise and Super Target Stores across 49 states and until recently has only built on large undeveloped/redeveloped suburban landscapes. The Target Atlanta Midtown at Atlantic Station store is one of the first of the new generation urban design strategy stores that began in larger cities such as Chicago and San Francisco. The Atlantic station site is 5.87-acres total with an available 4.86 buildable | parking area. 1.1-acres were un-buildable due to an underground utility easement. To achieve a store on this site we utilized a new strategy—a raised single level store over parking.

Yak & Yeti™ Restaurant Disney's Animal Kingdom® Park
Lake Buena Vista, Florida

Company: Landry's Restaurants, Inc.
Architect/Designer: Cuningham Group Architecture, P.A.
General Contractor: The Whiting-Turner Contracting Co.

Type of Merchandise: Restaurant

Yak &Yeti" Restaurant developed by Landry's Restaurants, Inc. and Schussler Creative, Inc. is a must-see restaurant experience within Disney's Animal Kingdom® Park. It complements the popular Expedition Everest—Legend of the Forbidden Mountain attraction by giving visitors the option of dining in an immersive sit-down Asian restaurant, visiting the theatrical quick service food café, or purchasing an item in the quaint retail village Yak &Yeti represents the first time a third party restaurant owner has ever operated inside a Disney Park. As such, close coordination between Walt Disney Imagineering, Cuningham Group Architecture, P.A., Landry's Restaurants, Inc., and Schussler Creative, Inc. was required. Design and development goals called for reflecting authentic Himalayan culture and eclectic Asian architecture while still performing efficiently to meet the demands of a large commercial restaurant. The design needed to blend flawlessly as part of Animal Kingdom's Asian-inspired setting and create a seamless guest experience by connecting existing establishments, all while not disrupting animal exhibits or current environments during construction. The resulting 17,366 squarefoot restaurant reflects the evolution of small houses and buildings stitched together over time to form a large dining venue at the base of the Himalayan Mountains. The immersive experience with 250 indoor and 350 outdoor seats both supports the existing park features and provides a compelling destination. Guests can dine in various rooms, patios and porches with well-designed sight lines allowing a full experience from any vantage point.

Winning Shopping Center Designs

32nd International Design and Development Awards

 International Council of Shopping Centers

About the International Council of Shopping Centers

This book is based on the information submitted to the International Council of Shopping Centers 32nd International Design and Development Awards program. Each shopping center featured in this book was the winner of a Design Award or a Merit Award, as determined by the Awards Jury.

The International Council of Shopping Centers (ICSC) is the trade association of the shopping center industry. Serving the shopping center industry since 1957, ICSC is a not-for-profit organization with more than 70,000 members in approximately 100 countries worldwide.

ICSC members include shopping center

- owners
- developers
- managers
- marketing specialists
- leasing agents
- retailers
- researchers
- attorneys
- architects
- contractors
- consultants
- investors
- lenders and brokers
- academics
- public officials

ICSC holds more than 250 meetings a year throughout the world and provides a wide array of services and products for shopping center professionals, including deal-making events, conferences, educational programs, accreditation, awards, publications and research data.

For more information about ICSC, please contact:
International Council of Shopping Centers
1221 Avenue of the Americas
New York, NY 10020-1099
Telephone: +1 646 728 3800
Fax: +1 732 694 1755
info@icsc.org (for general information about ICSC)
publications@icsc.org (for information about ICSC publications)
www.icsc.org

This publication is designed to provide accurate and authoritative information in regard to the subject matter covered. It is sold with the understanding that the publisher is not engaged in rendering legal, accounting, or other professional services. If legal advice or other expert assistance is required, the services of a competent professional person should be sought.

—From a Declaration of Principles jointly adopted by a Committee of the American Bar Association and a Committee of Publishers.

Published by
International Council of Shopping Centers
1221 Avenue of the Americas
New York, NY 10020-1099

BOOK DESIGN: Harish Patel Design, New York, NY

ICSC Catalog Number: 316

International Standard Book Number: 978-1-58268-087-3

Contents

About the ICSC International Design and Development Awards

The ICSC International Design and Development Awards Program was established to recognize outstanding shopping center projects and to provide information on them to the entire industry so that others may benefit from the experiences of their colleagues.

The 32nd International Design and Development Awards Program was worldwide in scope. Participation in other ICSC design awards programs, such as the Canadian or European awards, did not preclude eligible projects from being considered for an International Design and Development Award or Merit Award.

Projects that opened within the 24-month period from July 1, 2005, to June 30, 2007, were eligible for entry into this year's Awards Program.

Awards Categories

Categories for entries were:

Category A—Renovation or Expansion of an Existing Project
Entries had to relate to a project involving an entire shopping center, such as an enclosure, or a single facet of a center, such as an addition. The renovation or expansion must have been completed and the center fully opened for business within the 24-month period from July 1, 2005, to June 30, 2007. Eligible subject matter included, but was not limited to, improving the use of existing space, methods of keeping a center open during construction, new marketing and re-leasing approaches, refinancing techniques, innovative design and construction approaches, and adaptive reuse of the structure.

Category B—Innovative Design and Development of a New Project
Entries had to relate to a specific new shopping center, completed and opened within the 24-month period from July 1, 2005, to June 30, 2007, and must have demonstrated how a specific design or development problem was solved or how new standards in design or development were established. New methods of environmental enhancement, space utilization design themes, energy conservation and innovative construction techniques were among the subjects that were considered for this category. Entries included

detailed information about the design and development of the center, such as explanations of the reasons for, and the realized accomplishments of, the particular approach.

This year the International Development and Design Awards Program recognized the sustainability aspects and attributes of the various properties and bestowed a special award for Sustainable Design. Also, an award for Best of the Best recognized, from among the winners, the project that represented the best in design and development.

Awards Classifications

Entries submitted for either **category** were judged according to the following center **classification** system:

1. Projects under 150,000 square feet of total retail space*

2. Projects of 150,001 to 500,000 square feet of total retail space*

3. Projects over 500,001 square feet of total retail space*

4. Mixed-use projects and well-integrated developments comprising non-retail uses, such as entertainment, office, hotel, residential, sports venues and/or other uses that mutually support a substantial retail component.

*Total retail space includes all square footage included in gross leasable areas (GLA), all department store or other anchor square footage, movie theaters, ice skating rinks, entertainment centers and all peripheral (out-lot) space engaged in retail enterprise. It does not include office or hotel square footage.

Eligibility

1. The ICSC International Design and Development Awards Program was open only to ICSC member companies. Any ICSC member company could enter as many projects as desired in either of the two categories.

2. Entries must have had the authorization and signature of the owner or management company of the property.

3. Projects opened within the 24-month period from July 1, 2005, to June 30, 2007, were eligible.

4. Projects must have been completed and opened for business by July 1, 2007.

5. Separate phases of a project could be submitted individually, provided they were completed and opened for business by July 1, 2007.

6. Projects could only be submitted once. Projects that were entered in the past could not be resubmitted unless substantial changes were made since the last submission.

7. Members entering the ICSC Canadian or ICSC European awards programs had to submit separately to the International Design and Development Awards Program, and entries had to adhere to its entry guidelines and requirements. Entries accepted into other ICSC awards programs did not automatically qualify for this program, nor was any entry excluded simply because it was an award winner in another program.

If you have any questions about the International Council of Shopping Centers International Design and Development Awards, or would like to receive an application for the upcoming awards program, please contact:

International Council of Shopping Centers
International Design and Development Awards
1221 Avenue of the Americas
41st Floor
New York, NY 10020-1099
(646) 728-3462
www.icsc.org

Foreword

"We shape our buildings, thereafter they shape us," opined Winston Churchill.

As this decade draws to a close, there is no doubt that each decade brings its own design stamp. The hallmark of this decade can be described in one word, *placemaking*.

In North America, whether it is the new generation open-air mall, "New Urbanism" with its vertical mixed-use, "the Urban Resort" or the traditional neighborhood center, it all focuses around celebrating the outdoors. Creating an upbeat, stimulating sense of place surrounded by warm and inviting architecture and enhanced by alfresco dining and drinking underscores the new design paradigm. In other regions around the world, the enclosed mall infatuation still prevails but with exciting external design and animation. With uplifting curb appeal, projects are far more sensitive and appreciated in their local environments.

Across the board, the convergence of recreation, leisure, entertainment and dining as integral pursuits to shopping and vice versa becomes inextricably linked. As a consequence, the industry is responding with projects that are far more multipurpose in nature and thus reflective of changing lifestyles and aspirations. They have become the new village square—the social gathering place of the community.

As these centers continue to evolve and increasingly shape our lifestyles, we marvel at their inspiring influence. In this rising tide to be the best, such was the case this 32nd year where a record 65 entries were received. Twenty-nine were finalists, with Europe boasting more than half with 15 entries followed by 3 from Australasia and 2 from Latin America. What is extraordinary are the 4 finalists stemming from Poland, highlighting just how quickly global ideas and concepts become instantly transportable yet intermixed with the local vernacular.

As you review these award winners, you will observe:
- The clever adaptive re-use of factories, textile mills and breweries
- The breakthrough design in food courts with different seating, pedestrian flow and tenant mix creating an ambiance that is utterly different
- The continuing emphasis of blending the indoor with the outside environment
- The theater of fire and fountains as a means of inducing a crowd
- The drama of new ceiling and floor treatments combined with higher intensity streetscaping lending even more authenticity

This year, reflecting the zenith in design and development, an award has been given from among the finalists of the International Design and Development Awards for the "Best of the Best," the best shopping center to have opened in the world in this last judging period. That project is Westfield San Francisco Centre. In addition, ICSC has continued the tradition and an award has been given for sustainable design. This year's award went to ATRIO in Villach, Austria.

On behalf of my fellow jurors, I hope you enjoy reviewing these flagship projects as much as we did judging them. These award-winning projects are truly shaping our lives. They are a great credit to our flagship industry and thus exemplify such profound excellence.

Ian F. Thomas
Thomas Consultants, Inc.

Chairman
ICSC 2008 International Design and Development
Awards Jury

The International Council of Shopping Centers 32nd

Ian F. Thomas, CDP
Thomas Consultants, Inc.
Vancouver, Canada/Brisbane, Australia

Ian F. Thomas is chairman of Thomas Consultants, Inc., a firm specializing in the planning and development of large-scale retail projects around the world. They have undertaken projects in over 58 countries.

Mr. Thomas sits on ICSC's Board of Trustees and also the Foundation Board. In addition, he is the chairman of ICSC's International Design & Development Awards program. In 1989 he started the "Whistler Winter Conference," which attracts over 3,000 delegates. In 2002, Mr. Thomas initiated "The Leading Edge" Conference in Vail, Colorado, now called REvent. He is the recipient of ICSC's newest professional designation—Certified Development, Design and Construction Professional.

Arcadio Gil Pujol, CSM, CMD, CDP
LaSBA
Madrid, Spain

The managing director of LaSBA, Mr. Arcadio Gil's career in shopping center development and investment spans over 25 years. He founded Laese, a services provider, and was European director of the retail group at Jones Lang LaSalle. He teaches postgraduate courses, regularly speaks at conferences and seminars, and is a contributing writer to professional magazines.

A member of the ICSC European Board and the CDP Governing Committee, Mr. Gil received the 2005 ICSC Trustees Distinguished Service Award. He chairs the Spanish Council of Shopping Centres and is a trustee of the Fundecc, the Spanish SC Educational Foundation and a member of the Board of the Civil Engineers Spanish Institute.

Ronald A. Altoon, FAIA, CDP
Altoon + Porter Architects, LLP
Los Angeles, CA, USA

Ronald A. Altoon, FAIA, CDP, a founding partner of Altoon + Porter Architects, LLP, is responsible for the design of retail/mixed-use projects worldwide. He is a lecturer at ICSC conferences on global retail design trends and a University of Shopping Centers instructor.

Mr. Altoon's designs have received over 65 awards for design excellence worldwide, including 16 ICSC International Design & Development Awards, and an Asia Shopping Center Award. He sits on the NAAB visitation teams and the GSA's Register of Peer Professionals. He has authored *International Shopping Center Architecture, Designing the World's Best Retail Centers* and *21st Century Retail Centers: Context, Culture and Community*.

Gordon T. "Skip" Greeby, Jr., CDP
The Greeby Companies, Inc.
Lake Bluff, IL, USA

Gordon T. "Skip" Greeby, Jr., president of The Greeby Companies, Inc., has directed his company since 1978 providing development management, project management and tenant coordination services to developers and institutional investors worldwide.

Mr. Greeby is an ICSC Trustee and co-chairs the CDP Admissions and Governing Committee. He also chairs ICSC's U.S. Design and Development Awards Committee; serves on, and is past chair of, the CenterBuild Program Committee; is a John T. Riordan School for Professional Development instructor and University of Shopping Centers dean and instructor; and has received ICSC's Board of Trustees Distinguished Service Award.

Marcelo Baptista Carvalho, CSM, CMD
Ancar Ivanhoe
Rio de Janeiro, Brazil

Marcelo Carvalho is the co-chairman of Ancar Ivanhoe, one of the most preeminent shopping center owners, developers and managers in Brazil, with more than 35 years experience in the market. He is the president of ABRASCE—Associação Brasileira de Shopping Centers (Brazilian Association of Shopping Centers).

Marcelo is a member of ICSC's Board of Trustees. He also serves as the president of the Rio de Janeiro chapter of NGO Junior Achievement and is a member of the Rio de Janeiro chapter of the Young President's Organization. Marcelo holds a Bachelor's degree in Business Administration and is a graduate of the Owner/President Management Program (OPM) at Harvard Business School.

John M. Millar, SCSM
Divaris Real Estate, Inc.
Virginia Beach, VA, USA

John M. Millar is executive vice president of Divaris Real Estate, a developer of mixed-use town centers. He is responsible for the strategic planning, development and management of college town centers as well as the redevelopment of obsolete retail centers. Mr. Millar has also held executive vice president positions with General Growth Properties and Jones Lang LaSalle.

Mr. Millar has taught at ICSC's University of Shopping Centers and is presently serving on the ICSC Design and Development Awards Committee. Mr. Millar is also an Urban Land Institute member and has held leadership positions on several commercial retail councils.

International Design and Development Awards Jury

Richard Moses
RM/d
Woodland Hills, CA, USA

Rick Moses is the founder and president of RM/d, a full service development company specializing in mixed-use and retail projects focusing primarily on the California market. RM/d gained momentum as a "new" company with years of development experience as its foundation and has become a sought-after development resource and partner.

Mr. Moses has been the chief development officer for Caruso Affiliated in Los Angeles, heading up all phases of development on high profile mixed-use destination environments. He also held senior executive positions with General Growth Properties and Homart Development.

Kathleen M. Nelson
KMN Associates, LLC
New York, NY, USA

Kathleen M. Nelson is the president and founder of KMN Associates, LLC, a commercial real estate and investment advisory firm. Ms. Nelson served as a managing director/group leader for TIAA-CREF's Mortgage & Real Estate Division.

She was involved in the financing of TIAA's most prominent real estate investments, including most of the major shopping centers and mixed-use projects in the United States. Ms. Nelson is the first financial services representative and only the second woman to chair the International Council of Shopping Centers. She continues to serve on many ICSC committees, including the Executive Committee, the Nominating Committee, the Architectural & Design Award Committee, the ICSC Foundation Board and she is chair of the ICSC Audit Committee.

J. Thomas Porter, AIA, CDP
tvsdesign
Atlanta, GA, USA

Tom Porter is a principal at tvsdesign, an international design firm providing services in planning, architecture and interior design. Mr. Porter's designs include projects in South America, the Middle East, Asia and the United States. During his 37 years at tvsdesign, Mr. Porter has seen the practice grow to include retail, hotels, convention centers, educational facilities, cultural arts, office, and mixed-use developments. His practice specializes in retail design, but his studio includes all forms of commercial development.

Mr. Porter has been chairman of ICSC's CenterBuild Conference, a program committee member for the Mixed-Use Conference and the Open Air Conference and a member of the ICSC Awards jury.

Jeff Rossely
Premier Group W.L.L.
Manama, Kingdom of Bahrain

Jeff Rossely is a chief development officer with Premier Group W.L.L., a Bahrain-based investment and real estate development company. He has over 35 years in real estate development, with experience in retail developments, master-planned communities and hospitality.

Mr. Rossely has served as a chief executive officer at MAF Developments LLC in Dubai, United Arab Emirates, undertaking large-scale entrepreneurial and innovative mixed-use projects within the MENA region, including Mall of the Emirates and Ski Dubai. Prior to coming to the Middle East in 1998, he held positions as CEO in a number of major master-planned community developers in Australia, notably Robina Land Corporation on the Gold Coast and Honeysuckle Development Corp in Newcastle.

James P. Ryan, AIA
JPRA Architects
Novi, MI, USA

Jim Ryan is the founder and former chairman of JPRA Architects, which he founded in 1978. Although retired, he continues to act as an advisor for the firm's marketing, architectural design and business development activities. JPRA Architects specializes nationally and internationally in commercial retail projects, many of which have been distinguished with honors bestowed by the American Institute of Architects (AIA), International Council of Shopping Centers (ICSC), Urban Land Institute (ULI) and many other industry establishments.

A registered architect in 20 states, Jim is a member of the AIA, ICSC, ULI and NCARB. He has lectured at schools and universities and has served as both speaker and chairperson at various ICSC and ULI events.

Gerald M. White
Grubb & Ellis|The Winbury Group
Kansas City, MO, USA

Jerry White began his career with Copaken, White & Blitt as a tenant coordinator at Rockaway Town Square Mall in Rockaway, New Jersey. He was active in the leasing, development, marketing and management of major malls in the Midwest. In 2005, Mr. White conceived of RAAF, a real estate acquisition fund. He has also worked with national department stores and specialty retailers to achieve zoning approval and financial public-private partnerships in these developments.

Mr. White is currently with Grubb & Ellis|The Winbury Group in Kansas City and is an active broker and consultant, advising private equity interests on their real estate holdings. He is an ICSC past trustee, serving from 1988 to 1999, and a past chairman of the ICSC Foundation.

Advisory Committee

Rao K. Sunku
Raksha Consulting Inc.
Plano, TX, USA

Rao Sunku is a principal in Raksha Consulting Inc., providing planning and development solutions for retail, multi- and mixed-use projects. He has over 36 years of experience in retail real estate including planning, design and development. Previously, he was the director of site planning in the Real Estate Department of JCPenney Corporation, working with developers, architects and consulting engineers to achieve new locations and to protect company assets during the expansion and renovation process of existing centers.

Mr. Sunku has reviewed, analyzed and participated in the design process of over 500 retail centers in North America, South America and Central America.

Daryl K. Mangan
Retail Property Solutions, LLC
Atlanta, GA, USA

Daryl Mangan is a principal in Retail Property Solutions, LLC, a retail real estate advisory firm. He has over 30 years experience in retail real estate, including center development, asset management, leasing, operations management and marketing. Previously, he was COO of Colonial Property Trust's retail division and held leadership positions at Safeco Properties and Equitable Real Estate Investment Management.

Mangan has served as chairman of ICSC's Design and Development Awards for seven years, as an Executive Learning Series instructor and as a speaker and panelist. Mr. Mangan was a 2006 recipient of the Trustees Distinguished Service Award, in recognition of 25 years of service to ICSC.

Winning Shopping Center Designs

ATRIO

Villach, Austria

Owner:
SES Spar European Shopping Centers
Salzburg, Austria

Management, Development and Leasing Company:
SES Spar European Shopping Centers
Salzburg, Austria

Design and Production Architect:
ATP Architects and Engineers
Innsbruck, Austria

Graphic Designer:
ATP Architects and Engineers
Innsbruck, Austria

Lighting Designer:
Lichtlabor Bartenbach
Innsbruck, Austria

Landscape Architect:
ATP Architects and Engineers
Innsbruck, Austria

Gross size of center:
314,318 sq. ft.

**Gross leasable area
(small shop space, excluding anchors):**
160,290 sq. ft.

Total acreage of site:
14.5

Type of center:
Regional

Physical description:
Four-level enclosed mall

Location of trading area:
Urban central business district

Population:
- Primary trading area
  250,000
- Secondary trading area
  660,000
- Annualized percentage of shoppers
  anticipated to be from outside trade
  area: 10%

Development schedule:
- Opening date
  March 19, 2007

Parking spaces:
- 2,002

*ATRIO serves
customers from three
nations—Austria,
Italy and Slovenia—
and its design reflects
their languages and
cultures.*

Aerial Views: © Alpine Luftbild, Innsbruck
Photographs: © Thomas Jantscher

*L*ocated at the junction of Austria, Italy and Slovenia, ATRIO caters to their three cultures and three languages in a themed four-level mall. The center's conceptual model is *senza confini* (without borders), perhaps best illustrated at the mall's central plaza, where shoppers can walk on a huge aerial photograph of the area, strolling virtually from country to country.

With the design based on the classic Roman atrium, the plaza serves both as a communal center and a retail center. Shops along the mall are less deep and more visible than those typically found fronting a regional center mall.

Parking facilities include decks, a watertight parking garage and rooftop parking. Concrete paneled floors are removable for maintenance. The plaza's glass roof includes laminated timber beams of filigree and newly developed glazing with high transparency and low energy transmission.

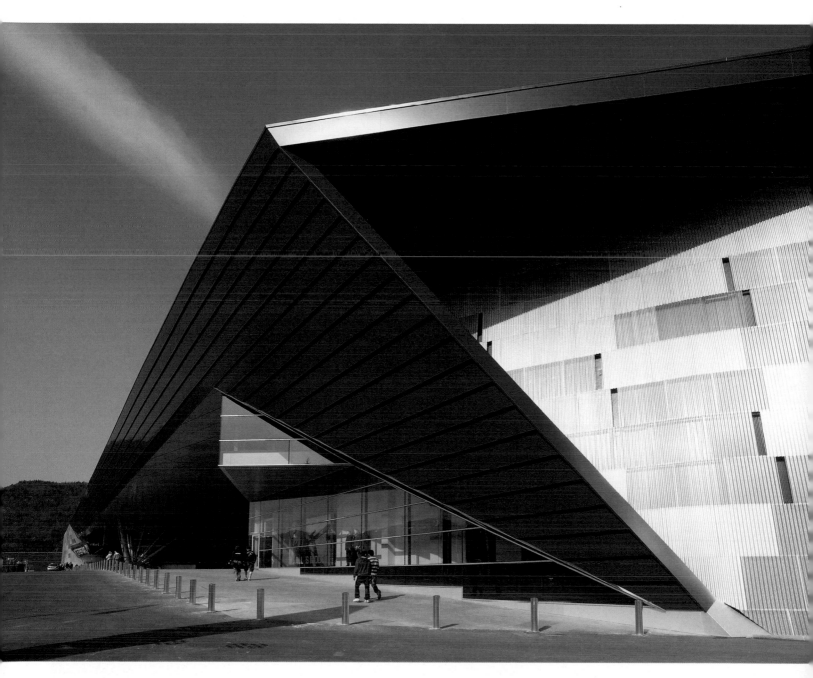

ATRIO seeks to be family friendly. Parking spaces are extra wide and a large play area—Capella Play—covers 6,500 square feet on three floors. All five restrooms include diaper-changing stations, and three contain special chairs for breast-feeding mothers. ATRIO provides free hygiene products for babies and free loan of children's buggies for shopping families.

Environmental impact was carefully assessed and incorporated in building design. Rooftop customer

parking and a semi-underground parking garage reduced noise emission to a minimum. The center uses sound-absorbing materials and barriers in the external delivery area. External lighting complies with current European regulations to avoid brightening the night sky and affecting insect populations.

Textured foil in the exterior glass skin of ATRIO offers (below) solar and ultraviolet protection.

Extensive use of
glass in a food court
(left) allows patrons
to dine in an airy
space.

The glass roof over
ATRIO's plaza
includes filigreed
timber beams and
high transparency
glazing.

A wall-less store-
front reinforces
the openness of the
center's design.

ATRIO's landscaping
(left) uses gravel, lime-
stone, tall grasses,
water and plants.

The lightness of
design is reiterated
in the glass ceilings
throughout ATRIO.

The innovative exterior design gets much attention at ATRIO.

MAJOR TENANTS		
NAME	TYPE	GLA (SQ. FT.)
INTERSPAR	Hypermarket	81,324
Kastner & Öhler	Apparel	38,262
Adler	Apparel	23,823
C&A	Apparel	18,184
Hervis	Sports	21,950
H&M	Apparel	17,517
Esprit	Apparel	3,809

The landscape architecture varies from what shoppers have come to expect. Instead of the grassy lawns found at most shopping centers, ATRIO uses limestone, gravel, tall grasses, water and plants from alpine and Mediterranean locales, again reflecting the three nations from which it draws customers.

Landscaping choices also saved water, a consistent goal in the center's resource planning. Elsewhere, to minimize water use, restroom washbasins use proximity sensors. Water falling from the roof is collected and allowed to seep into the center's grounds rather than incorporated into the public wastewater network.

To accommodate the poor ground at the site, the center is built on concrete piles ranging from 66 to 230 feet long and these, too, aid the environment. Many of these are energy piles that utilize geothermal energy for heating and cooling the center. The water circulating in these piles takes advantage of the steady ground temperature for heat-exchange purposes, using this natural temperature difference to heat and cool the center. Use of geothermal energy contributes to the saving of primary energy, as it is a source of renewable energy. This process eliminates greenhouse gas emissions as well as sound emissions, which often result from rooftop heating and cooling.

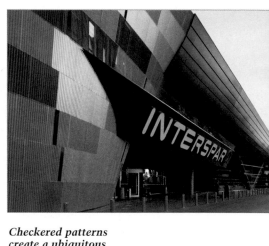

Checkered patterns create a ubiquitous design scheme for ATRIO's interior and exterior.

The center's architectural design makes full use of renewable materials. The mall's overscaled glass skin has a special textured foil that offers both solar and ultraviolet (UV) protection while providing an unobstructed view of the sky. The floors in both the plaza and mall are both covered in local stones: variegated granite on the lower floor to give a streetlike ambience and Gailtaler marble on an upper floor to lend elegance.

The system of separation and recycling commonly found throughout Austria governs waste removal. Anchor tenants deliver goods without packing and suppliers remove packing upon departure. Certified employees of the

center's management provide continuing waste-management training.

Other environmental enhancements came from bans on smoking on the construction site and in the finished center. Polyvinyl-chloride (PVC) flooring, resin-based floor sealant and synthetic paint thinners are all prohibited. Wood trusses are left untreated, steel parts are zinc coated (requir-ing no painting) and the exterior uses only aluminum and industrial coatings, needing no paint.

In every way—environmental, visually and retailing—ATRIO achieves its goals of serving three nations, three languages and three cultures.

Eye-catching (right) displays draw shoppers to ATRIO.

A large aerial photograph utilized in the floor design of Atrio's plaza depicts surrounding areas of Austria, Italy and Slovenia and reminds shoppers that markets are increasingly global.

Sunlight pouring through the glass roof illuminates design enhancements on almost every surface at ATRIO.

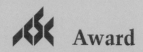
Branson Landing

Branson, Missouri, United States

Owner:
HCW, LLC
Branson, Missouri, United States

Management and Leasing Company:
Urban Retail Properties, Co.
Chicago, Illinois, United States

Design and Production Architects:
tvsdesign
Atlanta, Georgia, United States
Crawford
Branson, Missouri, United States

Graphic Designer:
McBride Company
Miami, Florida, United States

Lighting Designer:
Illuminating Concepts
Farmington Hills, Michigan, United States

Landscape Architects:
Butler Rosenbury & Partners
Springfield, Missouri, United States
Yung Design Group, Inc.
Branson, Missouri, United States

General Contractor:
Killian/Turner
Springfield, Missouri, United States

Development Company:
HCW Development Company, LLC
Branson, Missouri, United States

Gross size of center:
440,839 sq. ft.

**Gross leasable area
(small shop space, excluding anchors):**
261,632 sq. ft.

Total acreage of site:
95 acres

Type of center:
Mixed-use regional

Physical description:
Open air

Location of trading area:
Tourist market

Population:
• Primary trading area
  6,050

• Secondary trading area
  65,000

• Annualized percentage of shoppers
  anticipated to be from outside trade
  area: 70%

Development schedule:
• Opening date
  June 6, 2006

Parking spaces:
• 2,360

Branson Landing is a mixed-use project serving the 8.3 million tourists who annually visit Branson, Missouri, one of the major musical performance venues in the United States. The nature of the area presented the developers and designers with challenges and opportunities. There is a very small residential population catering to a year-round crowd of tourists.

Material resources are limited and the local labor market, small at all times, was being drained by feverish economic recovery brought about by hurricane devastation in the Gulf Coast. Nonetheless, the developers gathered sufficient labor and resources for the project, which provides 900 permanent jobs and has an annual economic impact of $300 million.

The center sits between a lake and Branson's historic downtown. Four mixed-use structures rise to five stories and shelter a central 2.5-acre town square. The structures include over 450,000 square feet of retail space, 106 waterfront luxury condominiums and a 243-room boutique hotel. Another 295-room hotel across the street supports a regional convention and tourism center.

The town square opens onto a lakeside boardwalk that contains a $7.5 million fire and water attraction. A brick-paved promenade stretches the length of the project, which contains 100 retail shops of which 70 percent are new to the

Branson Landing sits lakeside, near Branson's historic downtown. This mixed-use project includes retail, residential, hotel and convention uses.

MAJOR TENANTS

NAME	TYPE	GLA (SQ. FT.)
Belk	Department store	67,607
Bass Pro Shops	Sporting goods	64,500
Wedding Italiano	Theater/Restaurant	19,697
Coldwater Creek	Apparel	6,013
Famous Dave's	Restaurant	7,677

This Hilton hotel connects to the project's 220,000-square-foot convention center.

Branson market, including the first Belk department store in the market. A Bass Pro Shops anchor allows prospective buyers to test-drive boats on the lake.

Shoppers can take advantage of a full-size trolley car that winds down the promenade past 10 distinct restaurant formats, a children's play area with a nautical theme and access to public and commercial marinas. The project's town square can hold over 2,000 people for concerts and other performances.

There are six themed retail districts: the Station, the Wharf, Downtown, Uptown, the Neighborhood and the Country. Each themed area has distinctive architecture, wayfinding signage and a carefully crafted tenant mix. Teen and youth-oriented retailers, for example, dominate the Station while a seafood restaurant anchors the Wharf. Ann Taylor is found in Uptown, while a barbecue eatery and local souvenir shops are in the Country.

The project counts four major successes: urban revitalization, environmental improvement, creation

(Above and below)
Water features at
Branson Landing
enhance visitors'
experience.

Photograph: Illuminating Concepts

At night, tourists
can avail themselves
of Branson's famed
entertainment
venues or walk
through the center's
own downtown.

of civic space and economic productivity. The center achieved its urban revitalization goal by redefining the center of Branson, which had shifted toward the performance theaters west of downtown. With a viable mix of retail, entertainment, residential, hotel and conference uses, tourists began to add Branson Landing to their itineraries without drawing business from the performance venues.

To enhance the environment, the project's infrastructure improve-

(Left and below) A spectacular water feature integrates light, fire, water and music to entertain crowds at Branson Landing's Town Square.

ments ensure that all storm water runoff from downtown Branson is now filtered before entering the adjacent lake. Doing so unified a patchwork of irregular approaches to storm water management that had been degrading nearby properties. As a result, water quality and wildlife benefit from the net increase in urban density and lakefront activity.

Until Branson Landing opened, Branson had lacked a civic center. The project created civic space through its mix of retail, street

Small-scale design, sitting areas, gardens and ponds accentuate the downtown feeling of the project.

entertainment, distinctive light-water-sound shows and a place for public events. Economic productivity resulted from all that activity, and the variety of entertainment made Branson Landing a new tourist stop for those already in the area.

Branson Landing is a public-private partnership. Public investment made vital elements possible, such as the lakeside boardwalk, bridge and road access and the storm water filtration system. Private-sector investment drew national and local designers and experts in development, management, leasing and construction. The Missouri Development Finance Board provided $100 million in infrastructure bonds for public enhancements such as land acquisition, road and bridge improvements and management of water, wastewater and storm water.

With its scenic lakefront location and savvy mix of entertainment and retail, Branson Landing has become a tourist destination of its own within the already tourist-driven Branson market.

Photograph: Butler, Rosenbury & Partners

Photograph: Butler, Rosenbury & Partners

The children's play area (above) has a nautical theme.

Photograph: Butler, Rosenbury & Partners

Photograph: Butler, Rosenbury & Partners

A trolley (left) takes shoppers through the themed retail districts (above and right), which include the Station, the Wharf, Downtown, Uptown, the Neighborhood and the Country.

The boutique Hilton hotel (below) at Branson Landing sits along the lake

Photograph: Illuminating Concepts

Each storefront at Branson Landing makes its own statement, as if the project had evolved piecemeal over decades.

Entre Deux

Maastricht, Netherlands

Owner:
Fortis Vastgoed
Utrecht, Netherlands

Management Company:
Actys
Utrecht, Netherlands

Design Architect:
T+T Design bv
Gouda, Netherlands

Production Architects:
AMA Group Architekten bv
Maastricht, Netherlands
Exner Architects
Arhus, Denmark

General Contractor:
Cordeel
Zwijndrecht, Netherlands

Development Company:
Multi Vastgoed bv
Gouda, Netherlands

Leasing Companies:
Multi Vastgoed bv
Gouda, Netherlands
3W Vastgoed bv
Maastrict, Netherlands

Gross size of center:
129,167 square feet

**Gross leasable area
(small shop space, excluding anchors):**
129,167 square feet

Total acreage of site:
1.6

Type of center:
Inner city

Physical description:
Three-level center

Location of trading area:
Urban central shopping district

Population:
- Primary trading area
  160,000
- Secondary trading area
  400,000
- Annualized percentage of shoppers
  anticipated to be from outside trade
  area: 55%

Development schedule:
- Opening date
  November 24, 2006

Parking spaces:
- 200

*Entre Deux in the
Netherlands combines
historic buildings
(including a thir-
teenth-century church)
with new structures
to create a retail
experience that
respects the past.*

*E*ntre Deux is an inner-city redevelopment project in the heart of
the shopping district of
Maastricht, the Netherlands, an
old city on UNESCO's World
Heritage list. The city center
attracts 15 million visitors each
year from the Netherlands,
Europe and overseas.

The Entre Deux project includes
the old (six historic buildings and
a former church) and the new (31
retail tenants and 19 luxury apartments). There were two major

design problems. The first came
from the variations in height
between two entrance areas.
Designers named two shopping
levels (one for each entrance)
"ground floors," with each offering equal retail experiences.

The integration of new construction in the old fabric of the city
presented another design problem.
The center is entwined with the
historic city center and unites
Maastricht's two most important
city squares. Despite its signifi-

The plot diagram (above) indicates how the new structures fit into the historic district.

cance, the area had been an eyesore. Protecting the historic buildings and improving the surrounding area required careful planning and construction and close communication between all involved parties: the municipality, contractor, developers, tenants, architects and advisors. The cooperation led to the preservation of the area's historic buildings. The Dominican Church, dating from 1291, and its irreplaceable frescos have become the highlight of the area—the building is now used as a bookstore.

Designers sought to blend the center into the surrounding community. The project includes 19 dwellings around a green garden. Shoppers can park their vehicles on two levels of underground lots. Use of local building materials such as Muschelkalk natural stone helps create cohesion between the old and new, although the natural stone was prefabricated in big pieces so construction time could be shortened. Developers demolished one old building not considered of historic value, but its concrete bricks became a source of new concrete for the Entre Deux building, saving resources.

Close cooperation between all parties created a compatible blend of new and old architecture (above and left).

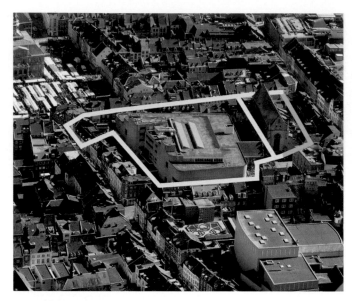

*Location of retail
and residential uses
are shown in aerial
photographs.*

*Sunlight streaming
in from above rein-
forces the concept
of open city streets
within the enclosed
space.*

Planners built environmental concerns into every aspect of development. The design of the cooling system guarantees it never runs for only one tenant. The bigger scale of the cooling system makes it more efficient and thus saves energy. Rooftops are used to introduce a green element into the project, improving air quality. The project uses energy-saving glass and biodegradable cleaning materials. Designers saved a monumental tree next to the church and flowers on the old city wall.

The project includes other conservation measures. Gray water is delivered separately to the sewer system, even though the sewer system itself does not yet have the capacity to manage

MAJOR TENANTS		
NAME	**TYPE**	**GLA (SQ. FT.)**
Zara	Apparel	5,085
H&M	Apparel	3,035
Men at Work	Apparel	2,380
New Yorker	Apparel	4,350
La Place	Restaurant	1,805

Entre Deux incorporates history in its design to create a contemporary shopping experience.

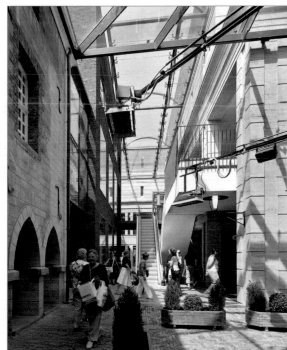

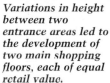
Variations in height between two entrance areas led to the development of two main shopping floors, each of equal retail value.

International retailers like Zara coexist comfortably alongside local shops, which often got top priority in the leasing plan.

One old building lacking historic value was demolished for the project, but its bricks were used in the new construction, further emphasizing Entre Deux's sensitive blending of historic epochs.

the separated flow. Tenants separate their garbage, with specific targets set, which is an effort encouraged by both the center's owner and the municipality.

Overall, the three shopping levels contain local food outlets, specialty stores and international fashion and design stores such as H&M, Zara, Mango and New Yorker. In some cases, local shops won leases over national and international companies, something the developer considered essential to the project's success.

At its opening, the Entre Deux owners gave a cultural grant to the city council, one of many successful initiatives to support the community. Entre Deux now attracts millions of shoppers each year, about 55 percent of them from outside the trade area. The project proves that modern retailing not only can exist in a historic district but also can enhance the area for the public good.

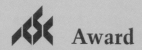
Manufaktura

Lodz, Poland

Owner:
Horyzont (subsidiary of Apsys Group)
Warsaw, Poland

Management Company:
Apsys Management
Warsaw, Poland

Design Architects:
Sud Architects
Lyons, France
Apsys Architecture & Design
Paris, France

Production Architect:
Sud Architects
Lyons, France

Graphic Designers:
Olivier Saguez
Paris, France
Virgile & Stone
London, United Kingdom

Lighting Designer:
Yann Kersalé
Paris, France

Landscape Architects:
Virgile & Stone
London, United Kingdom
Apsys Architecture & Design
Paris, France

General Contractor:
Budimex
Warsaw, Poland

Development and Leasing Company:
Apsys Group
Paris, France

Gross size of center:
1,940,733 sq. ft.

**Gross leasable area
(small shop space, excluding anchors):**
1,184,030 square feet

Total acreage of site:
67 acres

Type of center:
Superregional lifestyle

Physical description:
Two-level enclosed mall

Location of trading area:
Center city

Population:
- Primary trading area
  550,000
- Secondary trading area
  1.2 million
- Annualized percentage of shoppers
  anticipated to be from outside trade
  area: 12%

Development schedule:
- Opening date
  May 17, 2006

Parking spaces:
- 2,450

Manufaktura is in Lodz, Poland's second largest city. It sits on a 67-acre site that once held the former Poznanski textile mills until their bankruptcy in 1996. The center is organized around a 323,000-square-foot *rynek* (market square) and incorporates 14 historic 19th-century buildings with redbrick facades.

The main challenge in creating Manufaktura was refurbishing the existing historic buildings, which were in poor repair and had fragile foundations. Also, the mills were almost completely built on landfill, an inadequate foundation for the center. A covered river that ran through the site had to be channeled. A new road system had to be created to handle shopper traffic heretofore unseen in the area.

A design concept that amplified the redbrick industrial environment helped unify the new mall with the historic buildings. A simple linear design of glass and

Manufaktura (above) successfully refurbished nineteenth-century buildings (top) that had been used as textile mills.

Refurbishment of the site (above) included preservation of many local landmarks like the entryway below.

steel lent a contemporary look to the new structure, introducing modernity but respecting the historic.

The central public square and open-air parking lots required landscaping and lighting not normally found in industrial sites. To soften the harsh look of the manufacturing setting, the mall floors and outside decking are made of wood.

The mall uses an "8" layout with two levels that culminate in large open spaces. Defined retail zones attract various types of customers. One section focuses on children,

another on high fashion, another on popular brands and yet another on food and services. Major two-level stores anchor each section. Coffee shops and rest areas abound.

The two hypermarket anchors are at either end of the mall so as not to dominate the retail space for small shops. Many brands such as H&M, C&A and van Graaf have chosen Manufaktura as their first Lodz location.

Apart from its 305 stores, Manufaktura offers a wide range of entertainment and leisure options, including a food court, a

15-screen cinema with IMAX, bowling, climbing walls, discotheques, an aquarium, a casino, a gymnasium, medical services and a kindergarten. The center also hosts the National Museum of Modern Art and the interactive Museum of the Factory.

Manufaktura embodies the reclamation of under-used land. It has restored an inner-city brownfield, de-polluting the site and the underground river tributary. Since the buildings have historic value, the designers could not introduce aspects such as green roofing. The on-site woodlands, however, have been maintained and increased to ensure a natural and biodiverse environment. Water features and foundations now enhance the open-air spaces.

Whenever possible, the old buildings influenced the new, both as a nod to history and to address resource conservation. Local craftspeople undertook the refurbishment and used bricks from the demolished buildings as replacement pieces for damaged walls. Lapacho wood for the mall flooring came from a farmed sustainable source, and much of the ironwork in the original buildings can be found in the new structure.

A glass-enclosed building adds variety among the red brick facades that dominate the old mill fronts.

(Right) The mall's layout incorporates an "8" layout that ends in public squares.

Plazas provide public gathering areas for recreational and retail uses.

Manufaktura has a combination of cultural and commercial offerings to the citizens of Lodz.

Local stone and ethically farmed wood were used for external pavements, floors and decking. Landscaping included 600 new trees. All maintenance and cleaning products used on site are biodegradable.

While Manufaktura has been embraced by the community and shoppers alike, work on the center continues. Restroom facilities have been improved. More deck parking has been added. A dedicated public transport hub for trams and buses is being developed. A 278-room hotel, rooftop spa and conference center are being opened on the site.

Strong public-private partnerships, environmental enhancements and a respect for local history have made Manufaktura into a thriving enterprise.

Storefronts may be new, but their building materials reflect centuries past.

An interior hallway demonstrates how the old structure harmonizes with new design.

MAJOR TENANTS		
NAME	**TYPE**	**GLA (SQ. FT.)**
Real	Hypermarket	157,317
Leroy	Home center	116,746
Cinema City	Multiscreen cinema	56,115
Electro World	Electronics	38,447
Go Sport	Sportswear	19,450
C&A	Apparel	11,675

Some chains, such as van Graaf, chose Manufaktura for their first location in Lodz.

Developers took care to preserve as much existing greenery as possible.

Benches provide a moment's respite for shoppers exploring the sprawling layout of the old buildings.

Water features offer energetic design accents to Manufaktura's historic setting.

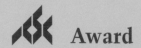
Waikiki Beach Walk

Honolulu, Hawaii, United States

Owner:
ABW Holdings LLC
Honolulu, Hawaii, United States

Management and Development Company:
Outrigger Enterprises Group
Honolulu, Hawaii, United States

Design and Production Architect:
Altoon + Porter Architects LLP
Los Angeles, California, United States

Graphic Designer:
RSM Design
San Clemente, California, United States

Lighting Designer:
Kaplan Gehring McCarroll Architectural Lighting
Los Angeles, California, United States

Landscape Architect:
Walters Kimura Motoda, Inc.
Honolulu, Hawaii, United States

General Contractor:
Charles Pankow Builders, Ltd.
Honolulu, Hawaii, United States

Leasing Company:
The Kaulana Corp.
Honolulu, Hawaii, United States

Gross size of center:
91,293 sq. ft.

**Gross leasable area
(small shop space, excluding anchors):**
91,293 sq. ft.

Total acreage of site:
7.9 acres

Type of center:
Fashion/specialty

Physical description:
Two-level open-air center

Location of trading area:
Urban resort

Population:
- Primary trading area
  118,000
- Secondary trading area
  900,000
- Annualized percentage of shoppers
  anticipated to be from outside trade
  area: 80%

Development schedule:
- Opening date
  May 18, 2007

Parking spaces:
- 371

*Waikiki Beach
Walk in Hawaii
restores a sense of
place to its section
of Honolulu.*

MAJOR TENANTS

NAME	TYPE	GLA (SQ. FT.)
Yard House	Restaurant	11,558
Roy's Waikiki	Restaurant	9,382
Ruth's Chris Steak House	Restaurant	6,288
Quiksilver	Specialty retail	6,214

The center (top) is surrounded by hotel properties. The Waikiki beach area's dense development (above) required construction managers to pay close attention to noise, traffic and waste management.

Indigenous plants and native materials strengthen the project's allegiance to the local identity. Displays of community culture (top right) are daily events at Waikiki Beach Walk.

Waikiki Beach Walk is a multilevel retail, dining, hospitality and cultural site in the Waikiki section of Honolulu, Hawaii. Waikiki means "spouting waters," and the area holds special significance to the islanders as the site of sacred healing waters. The developer sought to restore to Waikiki a sense of place, which he felt had been largely lost in the area's growth in recent decades.

The center's low-rise retail/entertainment complex sits streetside among four new or renovated hotel properties. Its evocation of Waikiki involves use of indigenous plants and tropical materials plus a commitment to culturally based programming and tenant mix.

The development process addressed several design and construction issues. One was mini-

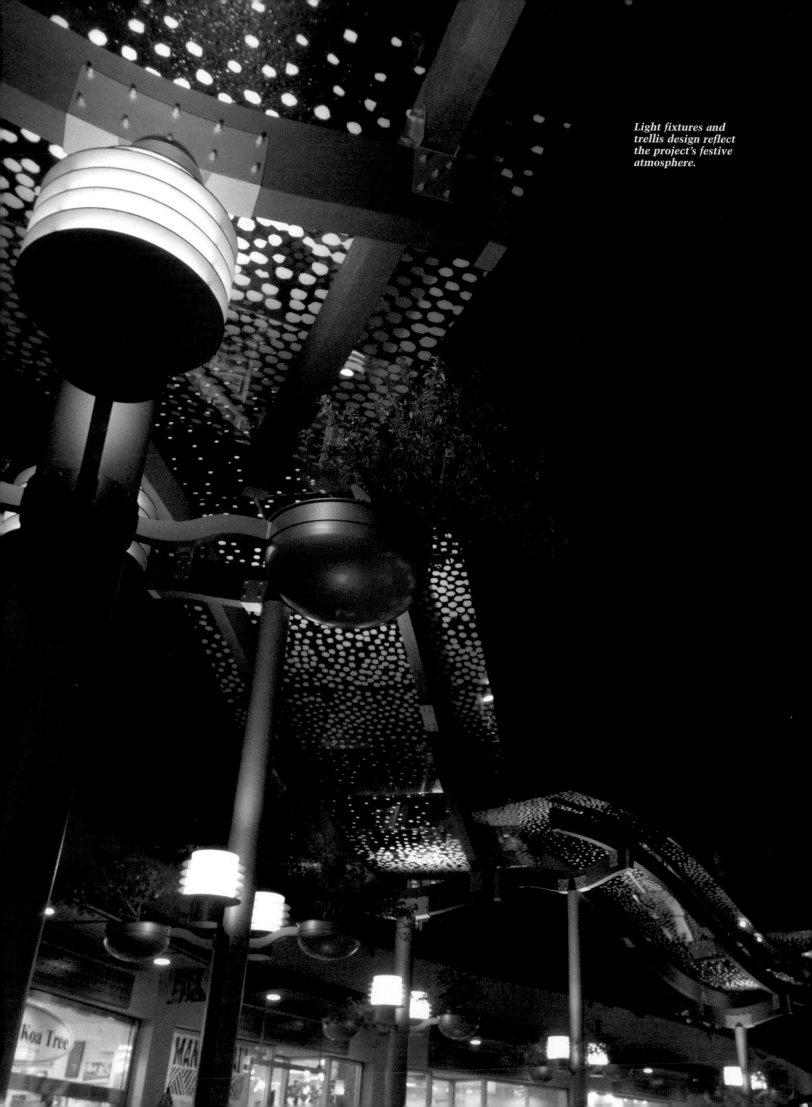

Light fixtures and trellis design reflect the project's festive atmosphere.

mizing construction noise and traffic impact on the surrounding hotels and businesses. The developer installed auger-cast piles instead of precast piles to reduced noise and vibration issues. This also eliminated the need for the delivery and storage of hundreds of precast piles, which would have been difficult given the constraints of both the site and the access points and exits. The recycling of demolition waste on-site for use as fill material cut truck traffic by 1,800 trips on the congested streets of Waikiki.

New infrastructure had to be installed around a labyrinth of existing sewer lines, drainage paths and utility lines (many of which were undocumented) without interruption to existing businesses. The development team created an elaborate construction sequence to enable new lines to serve as interim bypass systems while older systems were abandoned and replacement systems installed. Microtunnels allowed the installation of chilled-water central plant piping 18 feet below grade across two major roadways, avoiding costly dewatering and disruptive open-cut installation.

The challenge of recreating the Waikiki sense of place was met through a sustained immersion in local culture, coordinated by a cultural-awareness trainer. The eventual building plan was steeped in local legend, referencing Hawaiian god Maui's Hook. A quiet public gathering place is found deep in the site, well removed from the street. A progression of overhead curved glass canopies reminds visitors of the recurring tidal flow of Waikiki's spouting waters.

The municipality, city and the county of Honolulu were deeply involved in the project. Buoyed by the promise of new economic development and the area's restoration, the mayor's office and city council undertook $50 million in public improvements over three years. The developer and the authorities also worked together to ease existing regulatory barriers to development, establishing incentive-zoning mechanisms and creating tax holidays for real properties to enhance the financial

Waikiki Beach Walk transformed a deteriorating district into a vibrant gathering place.

Canopies (right) are common throughout the project, offering shade from the hot sun overhead.

While the project's design is Hawaiian, the tenant mix is international—below, an Italian restaurant in Waikiki.

viability of Waikiki Beach Walk's development.

The city's powers of eminent domain assisted in land consolidation. A special intra-agency project team led by the Department of Planning and Permitting helped streamline the process of permit application and review. The city's interactive "open-book" approach enabled the needs and expectations of both public and private sectors to be clearly identified and understood from the project's outset.

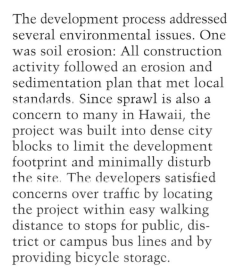

Hawaiian images from flora, fauna and nautical life are used on signage and design accents (left and above).

The development process addressed several environmental issues. One was soil erosion: All construction activity followed an erosion and sedimentation plan that met local standards. Since sprawl is also a concern to many in Hawaii, the project was built into dense city blocks to limit the development footprint and minimally disturb the site. The developers satisfied concerns over traffic by locating the project within easy walking distance to stops for public, district or campus bus lines and by providing bicycle storage.

The project's Hawaii-centric aim is also reflected in the tenant mix: 80 percent of retail tenants are locally owned and operated. Overall, the Waikiki Beach Walk satisfied the developer's desire to restore the Waikiki sense of place, local officials' hope for economic development and residents' need to sustain their high quality of local life.

Locally owned and operated stores make up most of Waikiki Beach Walk's tenant mix.

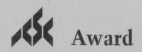
Zlote Tarasy

Warsaw, Poland

Owner:
Zlote Tarasy Sp. z o.o.
Warsaw, Poland

Management Company:
MACE Polska Sp. z o.o.
Warsaw, Poland

Design Architect:
The Jerde Partnership International
Venice, California, United States

Production Architect:
Epstein Sp. z o.o.
Warsaw, Poland

Graphic and Lighting Designers:
The Jerde Partnership International
Venice, California, United States
Epstein Sp. z o.o.
Warsaw, Poland

Landscape Architects:
The Jerde Partnership International
Venice, California, United States
Epstein Sp. z o.o.
Warsaw, Poland

General Contractor:
Skanska S.A.
Warsaw, Poland

Development Company:
ING Real Estate Development Sp. z o.o.
Warsaw, Poland

Leasing Company:
Cushman & Wakefield
Warsaw, Poland

Gross size of center:
685,028 sq. ft.

**Gross leasable area
(small shop space, excluding anchors):**
376,240 sq. ft.

Total acreage of site:
1.5 acres

Type of center:
Mixed use

Physical description:
Nine-level mall

Location of trading area:
Urban central business district

Population:
• Primary trading area
  1 million

• Secondary trading area
  650,000

Development schedule:
• Opening date
  February 7, 2007

Parking spaces:
• 1,600

Zlote Tarasy shopping center also holds two office buildings and a four-level underground parking lot.

Warsaw's historic urban parks inspired the design of Zlote Tarasy, a retail/leisure center within a mixed-use project in Warsaw, Poland. The project includes two office buildings and a four-level underground parking lot. The center blends organic architecture, urban squares, passages, green spots and water features. The concept is called "parkitecture."

A one-acre undulating glass roof is the preeminent architectural distinction of the center. The roof, which took two years to design and one year to build. The roof spans 394 feet, with individual spans of about 100 feet. The diaphanous glass canopy works to blur indoor and outdoor space and infuses the center's interior with natural light. It is composed of nearly 5,000 custom-shaped triangular panes of glass that fit into a self-supporting steel structure weighing 800 tons.

The center itself blends into central Warsaw's urban fabric. Its interior circulation path connects existing pedestrian patterns, linking the city's southern capital center to the business district on the north side. The project includes a small urban park, which opens to the retail and entertainment plaza and cascading terraces.

Beyond its thousands of square feet of public plazas, plantings and water features, Zlote Tarasy brings many retail uses into the city center: grocery and service outlets; brand fashions; cosmetics, health and beauty outlets; boutique and

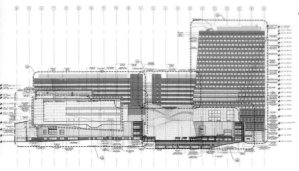

A side view (above) shows towers looming behind the retail area. Below, the lease plan illustrates the center's circular traffic pattern and shows the undulating roof centering above the retail floors.

MAJOR TENANTS		
NAME	TYPE	GLA (SQ. FT.)
Carrefour	Hypermarket	29,464
Marks & Spencer	Department store	27,586
H&M	Apparel	25,704
Royal Collection	Fashion	25,049

The iconic roof is visible from most locations inside and surrounding the center.

jewelry shops; electronics; accessories; shoes; sports items; and a food court, a cinema and a fitness center.

The project sought to integrate mass transit and pedestrian routes while improving the living quality of the area. One street was rebuilt with an underground infrastructure. An old tunnel leading traffic to the central railway station was adapted to the needs of the underground parking garage and public traffic. Reconstructed pedestrian paths around the building were enriched with greenery. A new bus station and more bus stops were built, and a new covered bus deck receives the majority of bus lines connecting the city center with its outskirts.

The center's underground passages now connect to those of the train station, enabling subterranean access to the mall. The project

Zlote Tarasy's office towers surround the shopping center.

improved the neighborhood's safety with round-the-clock security and 421 closed-circuit cameras. The center can depend on a two-minute response time from local police.

Environmental concerns played a large role in Zlote Tarasy's development. The city as a whole benefits from the reclamation of what had previously been abandoned space. The urban pocket park includes an 80-year-old red oak tree and 30 different plant species. The strong presence of public transportation and the air cascade system implemented in the building saves energy and improves air quality. Air is filtered before the center's system returns it to the atmosphere.

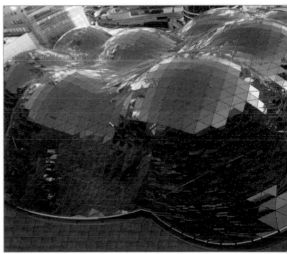

The roof spans nearly 400 feet, with individual spans of about 100 feet. Nearly 5,000 custom-shaped triangular glass panes comprise the structure.

The glass roof illuminates the center with natural light, saving energy. A "dusk system" turns on electric lighting only when the center's interior dims. Glass panels are fritted to eliminate the "heat-island" effect and ensure comfort for shoppers. Use of insulated glass prevents heat loss.

Natural light reduces illumination costs, while a frittered coating on the glass panels of the roof helps control interior temperatures.

The center segregates wastes and has its own compactors. Compressed wastes are collected by a refuse company. Fats and oils are separated from wastewater returning to the municipal system. Recyclable products and natural items accounted for 10 percent of construction materials. When possible, construction used local materials, especially for the glass in the roof.

While the unique roof may be an initial attraction to shoppers, it is the distinctive blend of retailing and "parkitecture" that encourages repeat visits from near and far to Zlote Tarasy in Warsaw.

Including parking areas, Zlote Tarasy stretches nine levels, with shopper movement encouraged by mid-mall cross-overs and overhead design accents.

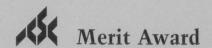

Briarcliff Village
Kansas City, Missouri, United States

Owner:
Briarcliff Village, LLC
Kansas City, Missouri, United States

Management Company:
Grubb & Ellis/The Winbury Group
Kansas City, Missouri, United States

Design and Production Architect:
Klover Architects, Inc.
Overland Park, Kansas, United States

Lighting Designer:
Yarnell Associates
Kansas City, Missouri, United States

General Contractor:
Meyer Brothers Building Company
Lee's Summit, Missouri, United States

Development Company:
Briarcliff Development Company
Kansas City, Missouri, United States

Leasing Company:
Red Development
Kansas City, Missouri, United States

Gross size of center:
101,678 sq. ft.

**Gross leasable area
(small shop space, excluding anchors):**
74,019 sq. ft.

Total acreage of site:
14 acres

Type of center:
Mixed use

Physical description:
Two-level open-air center

Location of trading area:
Suburban

Population:
• Primary trading area
160,000
• Secondary trading area
125,000
• Annualized percentage of shoppers
anticipated to be from outside trade
area: 35%

Development schedule:
• Opening date
October 29, 2006

Parking spaces:
• 605

Briarcliff Village in Kansas City, Missouri, is a mixed-use retail development offering boutique shopping, upscale alfresco dining, office suites and public gathering places in a modern interpretation of an Italian hill town.

The site has had a mixed history. The area was an enormous ravine 20 years ago, when a local visionary began the area's redevelopment by personally financing a highway interchange. With highway access, the donor filled in an 80-acre abandoned limestone mine with the hope of building a planned community on the site. Briarcliff Village is the epicenter of the planned community.

Overlooking the Kansas City skyline from a prominent 14-acre site that slopes 108 feet in elevation, Briarcliff Village comprises six structures, including a 600-foot-long main building with offices on its upper floor.

Photograph: Mike Sinclair

The site of Briarcliff Village in Kansas City, Missouri, slopes 108 feet. Its six structures include a 600-foot-long main building with second-floor office tenants.

Photograph: Mike Sinclair

A steeply sloping and intermittently rocky site presented the major development challenge. It required dealing with several subterranean geologic issues. An extensive network of caverns and remnants from past mining projects had to be filled and stabilized. Shale and limestone shelves had to be removed or partially removed and stabilized to allow for building foundations and piers.

Tilt-up construction techniques were used for the main building, which is made of cast-on-site concrete tilt-up wall panels, which reduced the cost of the building shell. Use of modular brick only at pedestrian levels and brick tile above saved additional time and

Old World Italianate storefronts (left) inspired Briarcliff Village's architecture. Bermed green spaces (below) lessen the visual impact of parking lots.

money. The facade also includes cast stone, simulated stone veneer, ceramic tile and stucco finishes.

The sloping site offered an unusual benefit: By using the grade changes, the center could offer on-grade access to the upper-level office suites in the main building, which increased demand for these spaces.

The architecture, inspired by Old World Italian storefronts, offers warmth and texture for boutique shops, clothiers, a jeweler, salons and an organic grocer. The largest tenant is a home-furnishings store. A cafe and a day spa enliven the tenant mix. The center boasts 100 percent locally owned boutique retailers and restaurants.

The center is embellished with sculpture, extensive landscaping and bermed green spaces, which minimize the visual impact of the

parking areas. Individual buildings are sized to match the Italianate design and the center's pedestrian scale as well as to enhance views from the second-floor office suites. The jeweler's building has a signature copper dome that also provides a buffer from highway noise. Two buildings form the vertical boundaries of a large piazza, which offers skyline views and contains a fire pit, sculpture, seating, a balustrade and Tivoli-style lighting. The piazza frequently hosts weddings, office outings, charitable events and other gatherings.

By offering upscale retailing, inviting streetscapes and a relaxed atmosphere, Briarcliff Village has become a popular site for summer concerts, movie nights, farmers' markets and special events, adding civic life to the retail project and laying the groundwork for the planned community to come.

Each building is sized to the pedestrian scale of its surroundings.

Stairways and passageways get full design treatment, as do plazas where visitors gather for a night at the movies.

MAJOR TENANTS		
NAME	TYPE	GLA (SQ. FT.)
Nell Hill's	Home furnishings	26,000
GreenAcres Market	Organic foods	9,396
Trezo Mare	Restaurant	7,712
Piropos	Restaurant	6,821
Tivol	Jewelry store	6,678

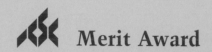
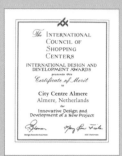

City Centre Almere

Almere, Netherlands

Owner and Management Company:
Unibail-Rodamco
Amsterdam, Netherlands

Design Architects:
Masterplan by OMA-Rem Koolhaas
Rotterdam, Netherlands
a.o. Christian de Portzamparc
Paris, France

Production Architect:
Beeking & Molenaar
The Hague, Netherlands

Graphic Designer:
Mission
The Hague, Netherlands

Landscape Architect:
DS Landschapsarchitecten
Amsterdam, Netherlands

Development Companies:
Almere Hart C.V.
Almere, Netherlands
Bouwfonds MAB Development
The Hague, Netherlands
Blauwhoed Eurowoningen
Rotterdam, Netherlands

Leasing Company:
Kroese Paternotte
Amsterdam, Netherlands

Gross size of center:
840,000 sq. ft.

**Gross leasable area
(small shop space, excluding anchors):**
650,000 sq. ft.

Type of center:
Mixed use

Physical description:
Two-level open-air center

Location of trading area:
Urban central business district

Population:
- Primary trading area
  187,000
- Secondary trading area
  225,000
- Annualized percentage of shoppers
  anticipated to be from outside trade
  area: 5%

Development schedule:
- Opening date
  April 2006

Parking spaces:
- 2,000

City Centre Almere is a mixed-use center in Almere, not far from Amsterdam in the Netherlands. Established in 1974, Almere is one of the nation's newest cities. Residential growth of 50 percent in 15 years had outstripped available services. No true city center had emerged in that time.

The mixed-use center contains 140 stores, a cinema, a music hall, a theater and a discotheque. The project rises from a number of levels. Below ground is a parking garage for cars and bicycles as well as access to public transportation and services. At the center's highest level is the City Roof Garden used by residents of the housing that borders the garden. Between these levels are the retail stores, which include anchors V&D and HEMA, as well as brands known worldwide such as Zara, H&M, Esprit, C&A, New Yorker, Mexx and WE. The Sting, a house of fashion brands, has been given a prominent position in the center.

Sixteen established architects contributed to the center's inner-city design. The project includes several smaller projects, requiring complex phasing of construction. The choice of high-speed construction called for prefabricated sections assembled on-site.

Mixing the uses provided some cross benefits, particularly for security. (The site is accessible 24 hours a day.) Placing residential units atop retail stores created a "neighborhood watch." Wide shopping streets and a lack of secluded areas have prevented

City Centre Almere in the Netherlands provides the first town center in an area of rapid residential growth.

As a public-private partnership, City Centre Almere needed to reflect retail and community uses (above).

Store and product names (right) call boldly to shoppers seeking to pair a retail experience with a day spent in the new downtown.

Green areas complement surrounding buildings, reinforcing the project's goal of serving as the community center.

Residential units atop retail stores (above) help enhance the center's security.

The tight urban setting required City Centre Almere (below) to move vertically whenever possible, freeing ground level space for community use.

vandalism. Stores have a "panic system" through which alarms ring in neighboring units. The nation's Ministry of Justice has presented the project with the "Safe Shopping Center" designation.

The project was a public-private partnership in which the municipality of Almere retained control of public space and cultural facilities. The municipality was also involved in financing up to the start of construction.

Environmental planning included a collective central-district heating system for all buildings. The vegetation in the roof garden is watered through natural means.

High-density site building preserved the surrounding Weerwater Lake and adjacent parkland.

Wastes are separated and collected through an underground refuse transport system. Organic waste, paper and residual waste are moved underground through a network of pipes to storage containers. Glass and chemical wastes are collected and stored separately for pickup. Cardboard is shredded at recycling points throughout the city.

Combining smart architecture with retail and residential uses has created a "city heart" that truly serves the people of Almere.

MAJOR TENANTS

NAME	TYPE	GLA (SQ. FT.)
V&D	Department store	99,000
HEMA	Department store	36,800
MediaMarkt	Electronics megastore	43,700
The Sting	Fashion brandstore	21,000

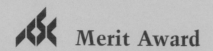

The Domain

Austin, Texas, United States

Owner:
Simon Property Group
Indianapolis, Indiana, United States

Management, Development and Leasing Company:
Simon Property Group
Indianapolis, Indiana, United States

Design and Production Architects:
JPRA Architects (Retail and Office)
Novi, Michigan, United States
RTKL Associates, Inc (Residential)
Baltimore, Maryland, United States

Graphic Designer:
JPRA Architects
Novi, Michigan, United States

Lighting Designer:
The Lighting Practice
Philadelphia, Pennsylvania, United States

Landscape Architect:
J. Robert Anderson
Austin, Texas, United States

General Contractor:
Beck Group
Dallas, Texas, United States

Gross size of center:
605,000 sq. ft.

**Gross leasable area
(small shop space, excluding anchors):**
385,332 sq. ft.

Total acreage of site:
57 acres

Type of center:
Mixed use

Physical description:
Open-air mixed-use

Location of trading area:
Urban but not central business district

Population:
- Primary trading area
  444,951
- Secondary trading area
  249,608
- Annualized percentage of shoppers
  anticipated to be from outside trade
  area: 13%

Development schedule:
- Opening date
  March 9, 2007

Parking spaces:
- 3,750

The Domain successfully combines luxury shopping with informal vibes fitting to Austin, Texas.

The Domain in Austin, Texas, is a mixed-use retail development offering over 685,000 square feet of retail space, 400 residential units and 90,000 square feet of Class A office space.

The developer also sought to create a "Class A" retail experience, one appropriate for luxury and high-end fashion tenants while connecting with the much-admired casual, outdoorsy and creative character of Austin. To achieve that goal, the designers chose materials, colors, tones and textures that complement and reflect the architecture of the indigenous Austin Hill Country style.

Planners gave high priority to the preservation of the site's century-old oak trees some of which exceeded two feet in diameter. They identified and transplanted particular tree clusters during construction. Spotlights illuminate these trees, which are protected with seat walls and naturally planted buffer zones.

The layout of the project was influenced by both the trees and by a 20-foot differential in a natural stone escapement. Well-lit paseos—passageways—give shoppers, diners, employees and residential tenants an increased sense of safety as they walk to and from their vehicles. The meandering configuration of Century Oaks Terrace results from leaving oak trees in their original locations. Further, the trees provide shade

Photographs on this page by R. Greg Hursley

Photograph: Paul Bardagjy

The meandering layout of the project's streets (left) accommodated the century-old oak trees on the site.

Photograph: R. Greg Hursley

Photograph: Paul Bardagjy

MAJOR TENANTS		
NAME	**TYPE**	**GLA (SQ. FT.)**
Macy's	Department store	140,000
Neiman Marcus	Department store	80,000
Borders Books and Music	Books and music	16,212
Z Gallerie	Home furnishings	10,000

Designers placed residential units above retail shops and met government guidelines for both affordable housing and leasing to local retailers.

Photograph: Paul Bardagjy

Photograph: JPRA Architects

for large sections of the retail street, while other areas are shaded by trellises and canopies anchored to the retail buildings.

Amidst the backdrop of the trees, there are both passive and interactive water features, fireplaces, benches, cafe areas and performance sites. The developer also engaged the nearby art community: Within the project, shoppers view the works of 21 local artists that include sculptures, wall murals and mosaic seat walls.

The project employed many types of construction materials and techniques: wood, steel and precast and poured-in-place concrete. Timely opening of the property required attentive sequencing of construction. Wooden residential units were built over the retail units' concrete base, allowing both uses to maintain their identities and structural integrity.

Local government laid down several rules for project approval. Within the residential component, 10 percent of housing units were required to meet affordable housing criteria. A portion of the gross leasable area was to be made available to local retailers. The

project included an outreach component to minority-business enterprises and women-owned businesses. The rules also required that the center generate at least 1,100 new full-time jobs. The project satisfied all these demands.

While a full-service hotel is currently under construction as part of The Domain phase I, Domain phase II plans call for several restaurants and additional vertically integrated retail/residential buildings on a 36-acre site. The second phase of this project, scheduled to fully open in 2010, will be oriented more to families and young people more than the first phase. It will also contain larger open-space areas suitable for public gatherings.

The Domain is serving as the catalyst for the total redevelopment of an additional 140-acre master-planned community under another ownership to the east of the project, demonstrating the positive impact of The Domain on Austin and beyond. New development components within the entire Domain complex are slated to open every year for the foreseeable six to eight years.

Photograph: Paul Bardagjy

Photograph: R. Greg Hursley

Built-in furniture (top) and wood flooring are comfort amenities.

Photograph: JPRA Architects

Front-in parking (left) puts more shoppers close to their retail targets.

Galeria Krakowska Kraków

Kraków, Poland

Owner:
Kraków Nowe Miasto Sp. z.o.o
Warsaw, Poland

Management, Development and Leasing Company:
ECE Projektmanagement Polska Sp. z.o.o.
Warsaw, Poland

Design Architects:
ECE Projektmanagement Polska Sp. z.o.o.
Warsaw, Poland
IMB Asymetria
Warsaw, Poland
Atelier Loegler
Kraków, Poland

Production Architect:
Strabag Polska
Warsaw, Poland

Graphic and Lighting Designers:
ECE Projektmanagement Polska Sp. z.o.o.
Warsaw, Poland
IMB Asymetria
Warsaw, Poland

Landscape Architects:
ECE Projektmanagement Polska Sp. z.o.o.
Warsaw, Poland
IMB Asymetria
Warsaw, Poland

General Contractor:
Strabag Polska
Warsaw, Poland

Gross size of center:
1,323,961 sq. ft.

Gross leasable area (small shop space, excluding anchors):
410,393 sq. ft.

Total acreage of site:
111.5 acres

Type of center:
Regional lifestyle

Physical description:
Seven-level enclosed mall

Location of trading area:
Urban central business district

Population:
- Primary trading area
  62,000
- Secondary trading area
  1.26 million
- Annualized percentage of shoppers anticipated to be from outside trade area: 35%

Development schedule:
- Opening date
  September 2006

Parking spaces:
- 1,385

The five-level Galeria Krakowska Kraków shopping mall reclaimed an underutilized site at the entryway to a historic district of Kraków.

Galeria Krakowska Kraków is a regional shopping center in the historic center of Kraków, Poland. Before its development, the site had been a wasteland—a chaos of bus roads and fast-food shacks—clearly unsuited to be the gateway to the city's historic past.

Developers faced extraordinary challenges in creating a modern retail facility while meeting the government's requirements of historic and monument preservation. Even the skyline of Kraków is protected as part of the national heritage, therefore the mall's design had to meet the government's strict rules to respect the architecture and scale of the surrounding historic buildings. A blend of sensitivity to historic practice and contemporary design resulted in original, diversified streetfronts finished with natural, high-quality materials.

The western facade, nearly one-third mile long, contains vertical divisions that mimic the rhythm

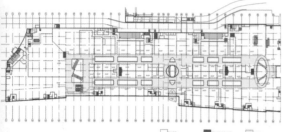

The contemporary interior design contrasts with the site's earlier use, which was marked by bus roads and fast-food shacks.

Apparel stores play a strong role in the center's appeal to area shoppers. Rather than being tucked away, escalators (far right) dominate the atrium, calling shoppers to upper floors.

MAJOR TENANTS		
NAME	**TYPE**	**GLA (SQ. FT.)**
Carrefour	Hypermarket	53,626
Saturn	Electronics	47,695
Peek & Cloppenburg	Apparel	38,158
H&M	Apparel	25,780
C&A	Apparel	21,289
Zara	Apparel	15,500

of a city street. Glass over the main entrance reflects nearby buildings and lights up the mall interior. Natural limestone, red travertine and recessed frontages split the facade into individual houselike sections. A clock tower dominates the facade and helps localize the entrances and tram stops of the historic center. Galeria Krakowska, the biggest building in the vicinity of the Old Town, sought to minimize the center's street-level impact by placing some of its parking lots on its top floors.

The mall's southern face is all glass. Its contemporary character emphasizes the historic railway station and post office. This facade is lit at night by colorful glass tubes that create unusual lighting effects.

Retail and transportation functions are interwoven. The mall is connected to a system of tunnels under railway platforms that will house the passenger hall of a future underground railway station. A tunnel connection also links Galeria Krakowska with a bus terminal located on the other side of the railway. A stop for the tram is located on the lowest level of the tunnel system.

Historic references influence the mall's interior design. The symbolic plan of Kraków's historic Old Town decorates the floor of "Hala Grodzka" plaza. One of its walls displays the motifs of arcades in Wawel Royal Castle, a Kraków attraction. Natural finishing materials associate with the old town streets. Two main malls lead from this historic plaza through a modern "Forum" plaza to a futuristic "Plac Europejski" plaza, which is the main passageway for shoppers and commuters to the trains and buses. The two malls were named after historic water and land sites in Kraków's trade area.

Plans included strategies for environmental protection and energy conservation. The center's public toilets are equipped with automatic water-saving switch-off taps. Efficient lighting equipment contains electronic upstream devices and the building uses a day/night control system. Building guidance technology allows managers to control energy levels during store hours. Use of escalators, ventilation systems and illumination are reduced to necessary minimums.

The success of the mall, with its 270 specialty shops, cafes and restaurants on three levels, shows that new retail can thrive even within the most restrictive of historic sites.

The two malls within Galeria Krakowska Kraków were named after historic water and land sites in Kraków.

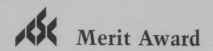

Merit Award

The O2

London, United Kingdom

Owners:

Anschutz Entertainment Group

English Partnerships

London, United Kingdom

Management Companies:

D3

AEG Live

Vue

London, United Kingdom

Design Architects:

RTKL Associates Inc.

HOK

Rogers Stirk Harbour + Partners

London, United Kingdom

Production Architects:

RTKL Associates Inc.

HOK

London, United Kingdom

Graphic Designer:

RTKL Associates Inc.

London, United Kingdom

Lighting Designers:

Spiers & Major Associates

Hilson Moran

London, United Kingdom

Landscape Architect:

Barr Gazetas

London, United Kingdom

General Contractor:

Sir Robert McAlpine Ltd.

London, United Kingdom

Development Company:

Anschutz Entertainment Group

London, United Kingdom

Leasing Company:

Montagu Evans LLP

London, United Kingdom

Gross size of center:
312,627 sq. ft.

**Gross leasable area
(small shop space, excluding anchors):**
115,960 sq. ft.

Total acreage of site:
31.75 acres

Type of center:
Theme/festival

Physical description:
Four-level enclosed mall

Location of trading area:
Urban but not central business district

Population:
- Primary trading area
  8.3 million
- Secondary trading area
  14.4 million
- Annualized percentage of shoppers anticipated to be from outside trade area: 30%

Development schedule:
- Opening date
  June 24, 2007

Parking spaces:
- 2,200

The O2 in London puts an abandoned landmark to new use as an entertainment and leisure destination.

The O2 grew from the unused iconic Millennium Dome, which was built by the British government to house the Millennium Experience, a major exhibition celebrating the start of the third millennium. The Millennium Dome closed after a year and the site remained unused for three years.

In 2002, an entertainment-focused company came to an agreement with the British government to open a world-class entertainment and leisure destination within the dome to be called O2. Designed, built, fitted out and commissioned in only 28 months, the property opened in the summer of 2007.

O2 has three sections. A 23,000-seat arena hosts live performances. An entertainment district features a mix of restaurants, bars, entertainment and retail and includes a live music club and an exhibition hall. Plans call for the leisure zone to be opened in 2011. The area includes an 11-screen cinema, nightclub and an exhibition hall.

Access to O2 is easy: It is located in a burgeoning part of London that is a five-minute walk from the subway and near London's light rail and riverboat. It benefits from the continued development of East London and the Thames Gateway and will be an integral part of the 2012 London Olympics.

To redevelop the dome, existing facilities needed to be stripped out. Building the new facilities amid the dome's structural wires and without tower cranes required major logistical planning. Piling through the decontaminated land was complicated, as was creating high-level bridges to permit servicing over a restaurant street. Specialists paid close attention to acoustics in building the arena

and were able to achieve four times lower reverberation than in London's famed Royal Albert Hall.

Interior design emphasized fun and fantasy. The spaces around the arena show a Miami-inspired Art Deco design aesthetic, with palm trees and a sugared-almond color scheme. Elsewhere, lampposts and benches reminiscent of Old Bond Street recall historic London.

O2 was a public-private partnership. The 150 acres surrounding

Photograph: RTKL Associates Inc.

and including the site are owned by the British government and have been leased to the project's joint venture entity for 999 years. The joint venture has leased the 32-acre dome site to the developer for 55 years, extendable for another century. The government collected no payment upfront, but receives 50 percent of all post-development profits. The project is part of a $10 billion master plan for the area, reclaiming 190 acres of former industrial land.

Originally, the developers had

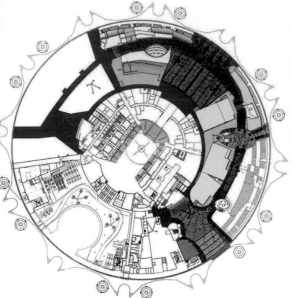

The O2 holds three sections —one for live performances, another for bars and restaurants, and the last, a leisure zone to be developed later. The dome's exterior (below) comes alive at night.

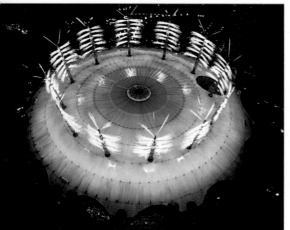

Photograph: Anschutz Entertainment Group

MAJOR TENANTS

NAME	TYPE	GLA (SQ. FT.)
The O2 Arena	Entertainment	2,624,672
Vue Cinema	Cinema	103,948
The O2 Bubble	Exhibition center	63,269
IndigO2 Music Club	Entertainment	60,000
Matter Nightclub	Entertainment	29,450

hoped to win the contract to develop Britain's first "supercasino," but lost it to the city of Manchester. The executives' concerns that they would have a harder time leasing the O2 retail spaces without the casino proved to be unfounded. In fact, they found that prospective tenants preferred not having the casino on-site and store lease rates soared once the casino plans were eliminated.

Despite the site's earlier failure, the developers of O2 showed not only how a space could be freshly reimagined to fill a market niche and generate revenues but also that large performance venues can serve as anchors in larger commercial developments.

Photograph: Morley Von Sternberg

The designers' concept emphasized fantasy and fun (above), including palm trees in London.

The Vue cinema at the O2 is a multi-screen movie theater, one of many entertainment options under the revitalized dome.

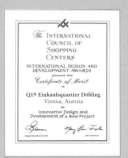

Q19 Einkaufsquartier Döbling

Vienna, Austria

Owner:
SES Spar European Shopping Centers
Salzburg, Austria

Management, Development and Leasing Company:
SES Spar European Shopping Centers
Salzburg, Austria

Design, Production and Landscape Architect:
peterlorenzateliers
Innsbruck, Austria

Graphic Designer:
peterlorenzateliers
Innsbruck, Austria

Lighting Designer:
Bartenbach Lichtlabor
Aldrans, Austria

Gross size of center:
110,000 sq. ft.

**Gross leasable area
(small shop space, excluding anchors):**
132,000 sq. ft.

Total acreage of site:
3.1 acres

Type of center:
Community

Physical description:
Two-level enclosed mall

Location of trading area:
Urban but not central business district

Population:
• Primary trading area
  54,000

• Secondary trading area
  112,000

• Annualized percentage of shoppers
  anticipated to be from outside trade
  area: 10%

Development schedule:
• Opening date
  October 2005

Parking spaces:
• 680

Q19 Einkaufsquartier Döbling in Vienna, Austria, occupies a century-old former paper mill that had fallen into serious disrepair. Its name comes from its home in the 19th municipal district of Vienna. Its central location and the high purchasing power of the market made it a prime prospect for retail development. As an early example of an armored concrete skeleton structure, however, the old paper mill was on a list of protected monuments. No development on the site could hide the supporting structure under cloth hangings and boarding. Rather, all the damage and repairs would need to be visible to shoppers.

The renovation of the facade of Q19, as it is called, was coordinated carefully with the nation's Office of Monuments. Sandblasting restored the texture of the original surface. Contractors used a process of concrete resurfacing that consists of spraying a light coat of mortar. A new outer skin includes a rear-ventilated facade made of corten steel plates. Vertically positioned round dome lights provide illumination.

The rough nature of the original structure's ceilings and walls contrasts with the polished Venetian plaster of the floor covering, glazing and display windows of the shops. People can now be seen shopping behind the windows of the old paper mill, energizing the mall's public areas.

Beyond the structure itself, the

Q19 Einkaufsquartier Döbling is named for its location in Vienna's 19th municipal district. It occupies the site of a former paper mill.

Shoppers arrive at
Q19 in many ways—
train, car, bicycle
and on foot from a
huge housing
project nearby.

MAJOR TENANTS		
NAME	**TYPE**	**GLA (SQ. FT.)**
INTERSPAR	Hypermarket	40,000
H&M	Apparel	15,000
Cosmos	Electronics	14,400
Hervis	Sports	14,200
Thalia	Bookstore	13,000

The mall's interior
shows modern
design, but the
exterior required
collaboration with
the nation's Office
of Monuments.

The glass roof (left)
contains awnings
that help reduce
energy used for day-
time cooling. After
closing time, night
air can be let in to
lower temperatures.

surroundings needed renovation as well. Across from Q19 stands the Karl-Marx Court, a social-housing project of the 1930s. To this day, it remains the largest connected social-housing project in Vienna, housing 1,300 low-rent apartments and nearly 4,000 people. Three-quarters of a mile long, Karl-Marx Court is also the world's longest residential building. Further, an unappealing park in front of the Q19 was redesigned. Working with the city administration, the Q19 developer created a master plan for the revitalization of the entire area. Green spaces were updated, lighting was improved and courts were built for soccer, basketball and beach volleyball. The developer says this was the first time a private investor put money into Vienna's infrastructure and public places.

Q19 is readily accessible. Surveys show that 50 percent of visitors drive to the site; the other 50 percent walk, cycle or arrive by public transportation. Parking spaces are eight inches wider than

required by law to accommodate larger vehicles. Shoppers have only a short distance to walk from their garage spaces to vertical access to the mall levels.

The development plan incorporated energy and resource conservation. If necessary, night air is let in to cool the mall after shopping hours. Lower outside evening temperatures also cool the sprinkler basin, which ensures heat exchange during the day. Awnings help reduce energy used for daytime cooling. Induction units reduce energy costs by about 35 percent.

Sorting of wastes encourages recycling and cuts waste disposal costs by 35 percent. The owner provides bins for paper, plastic, glass, metal, Styrofoam and leftover food. There is also a cardboard-box press and, for the caterers, an oil separator. In the mall area, separate bins for the various types of disposables allow shoppers to recycle as well.

Since its opening, Q19 has become a popular meeting place in the district, hosting many events by associations, schools, institutions and interest groups, demonstrating that even a damaged industrial site can become an appealing retail magnet.

Sharp storefront designs bring a contemporary feeling to Q19.

Natural light from above enlivens the food court (left) and mall areas (right).

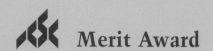

Merit Award

*Innovative Design and
Development of a New Project*

Salvador Shopping

Salvador, Brazil

Owner:
JCPM
Recife, Brazil

Management Company:
Salvador Gestão e Empreendimentos Ltda.
Salvador, Brazil

Design and Production Architect:
André Sá e Francisco Mota Arquitetos
Salvador, Brazil

Graphic Designer:
André Sá e Francisco Mota Arquitetos
Salvador, Brazil

Lighting Designer:
T. Kondos Associates
New York, New York, United States

Landscape Architect:
Benedito Abbud Arquitetura Paisagística
São Paulo, Brazil

General Contractor:
JCPM
Recife, Brazil

Development Company:
Construtora Andrade Mendonça
Salvador, Brazil

Leasing Companies:
Conshopping
Rio de Janeiro, Brazil
Saphyr
São Paulo, Brazil

Gross size of center:
592,779 sq. ft.

**Gross leasable area
(small shop space, excluding anchors):**
450,099 sq. ft.

Total acreage of site:
22.4 acres

Type of center:
Regional

Physical description:
Five-level enclosed mall

Location of trading area:
Urban

Population:
- Primary trading area
  383,800
- Secondary trading area
  849,900
- Annualized percentage of shoppers
  anticipated to be from outside trade
  area: 5%

Development schedule:
- Opening date
  May 22, 2007

Parking spaces:
- 4,200

*The site of Salvador
Shopping in Brazil
was transformed from
an eyesore to an
innovative, efficient
shopping center.*

Salvador Shopping is a regional mall in the city of Salvador on Brazil's northeast coast. Its three shopping levels contain 227 stores, including a supermarket and department store and entertainment anchors. There are two parking levels connected to the surrounding roadway system through three vehicular access roads and three pedestrian access points.

The project lies on the site of a former concrete factory, which generated noise and dust and left a harmful visual impact on the densely occupied environs. The factory's storage tanks attracted disease-transmitting insects. Crews broke up concrete found at the site and buried it in city-approved landfills. They also controlled noise during construction and made sure dust did not contaminate a drainage canal at the rim of the site.

The entire mall area lies under a transparent roof marked by spatial metallic arches of different styles and heights. The ceiling—nearly 60 feet high—can be seen from the ground floor, allowing visual integration of the shopping levels. Panoramic elevators, escalators and conveyors provide vertical movement.

The third floor houses an eight-screen movie theater, an amusement park with electronic rides

and a food court, which is surrounded by verandas that bring natural light to those dining. A space named Restaurants Boulevard unifies the food court's eateries, each of which has its own decor and service areas. Four larger and more sophisticated restaurants are found in the first floor's Gourmet Space, which is architecturally distinct from the rest of the center and offers alternative direct parking access and extended hours of operation.

Inside Salvador Shopping, a traditional floor plan is enhanced by a wide mall area, which includes sitting sections.

Anchor stores are found at each end of the center. Ten megastores are placed strategically throughout the mall to drive traffic.

MAJOR TENANTS

NAME	TYPE	GLA (SQ. FT.)
Cinemark	Multiscreen theater	44,784
Riachuelo	Department store	56,078
Renner	Department store	35,815
Bompreço	Supermarket	34,686
C&A	Department store	34,673
Game Station	Amusement park	15,878

The vast ceiling— nearly 60 feet high— is visible from all mall levels and draws shoppers to upper floors.

The two floors of retail units are laid out longitudinally, each floor having one anchor store at each end. Ten megastores are placed strategically, with five on each floor. Among the stores are 64 that introduced their brands to the city. A service operations court located near an exit offers conveniences to shoppers arriving or leaving the center.

Though situated in the most important business district in Salvador, the site nonetheless presented challenges. There was no road infrastructure around the site, and the soil conditions made construction precarious. The developer invested about US $20 million to build access roads on 62 acres in 20 months. Three bridges were built over a canal. One is used exclusively by pedestrians, who may also use three elevated footbridges. There are also two passages for vehicles,

three sewerage stations and over 8,000 feet of public pathways.

The new infrastructure includes drainage, lighting and other utilities, the design of which was subject to approval by the public authorities although it was paid for by the developer and donated to the city. Air quality and temperature are managed through a system that involves ice-cold-water variable flow, energy retrievers and air filtration. The electric system was designed for its energy efficiency, including the constant stream of sunlight through the domed roof.

All these components have merged to provide shoppers with food, retail and entertainment options in a comfortable environment at Salvador Shopping.

Dramatic design (above) draws attention to what might otherwise be utilitarian uses such as stairways.

Among the 227 stores are 64 that chose Salvador Shopping for their first unit in the city.

San Luis Shopping
Quito, Ecuador

Owner:
Centro Comercial Los Chillos S.A.
Quito, Ecuador

Management, Development and Leasing Company:
DK Management Services S.A.
Quito, Ecuador

Design Architects:
Michel Deller, John Clark, Guillermo López and Pipat Esara
Quito, Ecuador

Production and Landscape Architect:
Ekron Construcciones S.A.
Quito, Ecuador

Graphic and Lighting Designer:
Ekron Construcciones S.A.
Quito, Ecuador

General Contractor:
Ekron Construcciones S.A.
Quito, Ecuador

Gross size of center:
650,000 sq. ft.

**Gross leasable area
(small shop space, excluding anchors):**
350,000 sq. ft.

Total acreage of site:
15.3 acres

Type of center:
Regional

Physical description:
Four-level mall and town center

Location of trading area:
Urban but not central business district

Population:
- Primary trading area
  320,000
- Secondary trading area
  500,000
- Annualized percentage of shoppers
  anticipated to be from outside trade
  area: 20%

Development schedule:
- Opening date
  November 2006

Parking spaces:
- 1,500

San Luis Shopping is in the Los Chillos Valley area of Quito, the capital city of Ecuador. Two centuries ago, the vicinity held the nation's most important haciendas, whose lands over the years have largely been sold for commercial and residential purposes. The architecture of San Luis Shopping recreates that of the haciendas, with its thick walls, stone floors, hand-forged iron and many other details. The cool air of the Andes flows freely through the center.

In front of the retail project lies the San Luis Town Center plaza, which models itself on the United States town centers built in recent years. Its tower, about 130 feet high, can be seen from afar and is increasingly recognized as the icon for the entire valley. In addition to the mall stores, the town center will soon contain offices, homes, a church, a hospital and a home for the elderly.

Designing the project to resemble the haciendas of old was no easy

The designers of San Luis Shopping in Quito modeled their work on the large haciendas that once dominated the area.

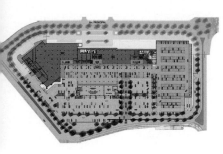

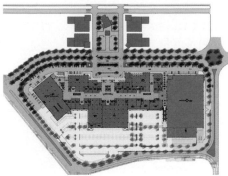

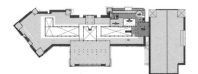

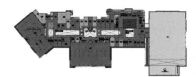

The area's first hypermarket anchors the mall's tenant plan (left).

Environmental protection informed the decisions of the developer and designers. Endemic flora was kept in a protected area. An artificial lake created 200 years ago was preserved in toto. The center has over 60 parking spaces for bicycles and motorcycles, all near the mall entrances. Mall employees benefit from changing rooms, showers, toilets and diaper-changing stations. One system reclaims water for drinking and another treats sewage for reuse to water the gardens. Water recycling approaches 100 percent.

task, since there were no existing patterns of that nature. Long periods of research included finding the right artisans—iron forgers, carpenters, stone craftspeople, etc.—to make the floors, doors, lamps, pots and other design elements. The artisans were then trained in how to create the highest quality in each piece to be produced. Some of the mall's artisans were the offspring of those who had actually built the haciendas.

The food court has a movable ceiling so families can enjoy meals alfresco on sunny days. Balconies, terraces and indoor and outdoor plants purify the air without use of mechanical devices. All construction materials came from the region, as did all construction workers. The building foundation used material from the demolition of old structures on the site. Trash is sorted on-site for recycling.

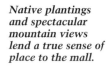

Native plantings and spectacular mountain views lend a true sense of place to the mall.

The hypermarket, not previously found in the area, was opened first, to provide supermarket services to the community. The developer later felt that the early opening of the hypermarket may have been a marketing miscalculation, since it detracted from the subsequent impact of the larger shopping mall. It also taught shoppers to enter the mall through the hypermarket entrance, possibly reducing shopper traffic to the other retailers. The developer solved this issue creatively by designing promotional events that drew customers through the entire mall.

The striking architecture of the project has subsequently become a reference for the development of an airport in a nearby city, testifying to the center's success in reclaiming the beauty of the traditional haciendas of Los Chillos.

(Left) Skilled local artisans such as iron forgers, stone craftspeople and carpenters were employed to recreate design features reminiscent of old haciendas.

MAJOR TENANTS		
NAME	**TYPE**	**GLA (SQ. FT.)**
De Prati	Department store	88,265
Megamaxi	Hypermarket	88,264
Ferrisariato	Hardware store	59,636
Super Cines	Multiscreen theater	44,035
Jugueton	Toy store	16,707

The hacienda influence is felt both outside and in.

Sihlcity
Zurich, Switzerland

Owner:
Investor Consortium Sihlcity, Zurich
Zurich, Switzerland

Management and Leasing Company:
Investor Consortium Sihlcity, Zurich
Zurich, Switzerland

Design and Production Architect:
Theo Hotz AG
Zurich, Switzerland

Graphic Designer:
Theo Hotz AG
Zurich, Switzerland

Lighting Designer:
Reflexion AG
Zurich, Switzerland

Landscape Architect:
Raderschlall Landschaftsarchitekten AG
Meilen, Switzerland

General Contractor:
Karl Steiner AG
Zurich, Switzerland

Development Company:
Karl Steiner AG
Zurich, Switzerland

Gross size of center:
441,300 sq. ft.

**Gross leasable area
(small shop space, excluding anchors):**
247,500 sq. ft.

Total acreage of site:
24 acres

Type of center:
Mixed use

Physical description:
Five-level open-air center

Location of trading area:
Urban but not central business district

Population:
- Primary trading area
  450,000

- Secondary trading area
  1.5 million

- Annualized percentage of shoppers
  anticipated to be from outside trade
  area: 5%

Development schedule:
- Opening date
  March 22, 2007

Parking spaces:
- 850

Sihlcity describes itself as Zurich, Switzerland's first urban entertainment center, hosting 14 food outlets, 81 retail shops, 16 residential units, a 132-room hotel, eight conference halls and a 10-screen cinema. There is also a club, a culture house, a fitness center, a health center, a church, a children's play area and a library.

The mixed-use project transforms and revitalizes a former industrial site, the Sihl paper factory, though remnants of old structures remain. The old brick factory,

which dates back to 1836, over-looks a large plaza. The factory's chimney, from 1912, has become a Sihlcity landmark. Designers exhausted the permitted degree of site utilization, but nonetheless created an open-air public-access-ible space suitable for relaxation.

The center's largest anchor ten-ants—who also have the highest frequency of shopper visits—are placed so that visitors walk past other stores to move from one anchor to another. Shopper traffic also comes from Sihlcity's place-

ment between the Wiedikon urban quarter and the nearby Allmend recreational area. More than 70 percent of Sihlcity's visitors arrive by public transportation—a per-centage high even by Swiss stan-dards, which typically sees 10 per-cent of visitors on foot or mass transit. Sihlcity is accessible to 450,000 people within 10 minutes' travel time and 1.5 million within 20 minutes. Railway lines, tram-lines and bus lines all serve the site.

The site is open at all hours. The mall stores are open from 9 A.M.

Reclining objects outside Sihlcity in Zurich work both as art and for a moment's respite.

The site (left) was once used as a paper factory and a few of the old structures remain today.

The entire Sihlcity is traffic-free at the above-ground level, with all the deliveries for every store carried out at the sub-terranean level.

to 8 P.M. six days per week, longer than usual in Switzerland, to accommodate the lifestyle theme of the property.

Energy plans kept economy in mind. There is a heating/cooling network that uses groundwater as environmental energy. Energy is recovered through the refrigeration, ventilation and air-conditioning systems. The building's insulation corresponds to the high Swiss standards. The waste-disposal policies at the center require tenants to separate waste and provide facilities where retailers can do so.

Government officials have certified that Sihlcity is free of any environmental hazards. Greenery covers over five rooftop acres, creating new habitats for birds and insects. Foliage covers a good portion of the property. The project did not contribute to urban sprawl, since it reused an existing

industrial site. Roughly 35,000 tons of excavated material was recycled and used in project construction.

In addition to its retail and entertainment functions, Sihlcity is home to several nonprofit organizations, such as a library and a church. A private foundation that aids people with disabilities and socially disadvantaged people runs the center's home-delivery service, which is unique within Zurich. Shoppers can arrange to have their Sihlcity purchases delivered within the Zurich city limits for a nominal charge.

Sihlcity has capitalized on what it calls "Swiss qualities"—population density, strong purchasing power, high ecological standards and advanced spatial and traffic policies—to create a small city within a city that can serve as a model for other European projects.

The Coop City department store (right) is one of three large anchors.

Some foreign retailers were so impressed by Sihlcity that they launched their market presence in Switzerland there.

MAJOR TENANTS		
NAME	TYPE	GLA (SQ. FT.)
Coop City	Department store	43,100
Media Markt	Electronics	43,100
Peek & Cloppenburg	Apparel	43,100
Ochsner Sport	Sports	23,700
C&A	Apparel	21,500
Zara	Apparel	18,300

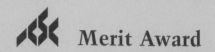

Southlands Town Center

Aurora, Colorado, United States

Owner:
Black Rock
New York, New York, United States

Management and Development Company:
Alberta Development Partners
Aurora, Colorado, United States

Design Architects:
Callison
Seattle, Washington, United States
Communication Arts, Inc.
Boulder, Colorado, United States

Production Architect:
Callison
Seattle, Washington, United States

Graphic Designer:
Communication Arts, Inc.
Boulder, Colorado, United States

Lighting Designer:
JK Design Group
Van Nuys, California, United States

Landscape Architect:
MESA Design Group
Dallas, Texas, United States

General Contractor:
Beck Construction
Dallas, Texas, United States

Leasing Company:
David Hicks and Lampert
Greenwood Village, Colorado, United States

Gross size of center:
613,000 sq. ft.

**Gross leasable area
(small shop space, excluding anchors):**
244,137 sq. ft.

Total acreage of site:
300 acres

Type of center:
Mixed use

Physical description:
Two-level open-air center

Location of trading area:
Suburban

Population:
- Primary trading area
271,519

- Secondary trading area
719,773

- Annualized percentage of shoppers
anticipated to be from outside trade
area: 2%

Development schedule:
- Opening date
October 20, 2006

Parking spaces:
- 2,192

*The design of
Southlands Town
Center mimics the
"Main Streets" of
the Midwestern
United States,
including the tradi-
tional downtown
movie theater.*

Southlands Town Center is the retail/lifestyle component of Colorado's largest mixed-use project. It covers 1.7 million square feet of space in the city of Aurora, which—despite becoming Colorado's third-largest city—did not have a defined downtown. In its 300 acres, the mixed-use project includes 443,000 square feet of retail space and 170,000 square feet of office space and has become the new town center.

Architecturally, Southlands Town Center is a modern interpretation of the classic Midwestern "Main Streets." On its gently sloping site, there are 21 buildings, each one or two stories tall. There are four blocks of retail, sidewalk cafes and second-level office spaces, plus a cinema and plazas. A town square hosts events year-round, such as a twice-weekly farmers' market in summer and ice-skating in winter.

Designed to look as though it had been built over time, the town

Photograph: Steve Crecilius

Photograph: Steve Crecilius

Photograph: Callison/Chris Eden

Photograph: Steve Crecilius

center blends traditional and contemporary architectural forms, natural and modern materials and colors and mature landscaping. A simple masonry palette, including stone veneer, brick and concrete blocks, helped create a wide variety of facade styles.

The biggest architectural challenge the designers faced was to maintain the Main Street concept throughout the 21 buildings on the sloping site while meeting the display and storefront needs of the individual retailers. To do so, the design team collaborated with the owner, contractor and civil engineers to develop a flexible building system that worked well with a cut-and-fill approach to balance the site but still provided enough slope to the street to offer a dynamic arrival experience.

The public spaces in the project have distinctive features, such as a central fire pit, carillons, feature planters, an iconic clock tower, sculptures and water features. The 73 stores in the center, including a large restaurant component, are mixed in with the public spaces to sustain the Main Street dynamic. Lights strung across the streets lend a holiday atmosphere year round. Children are welcome to cavort on the interactive water features. The drivable streets include diagonal parking in front of stores.

Intense collaboration marked every phase of development: between the owner and the city, the owner and designers, the designers with each other, and among the design, construction and leasing teams. Construction costs were higher than for an enclosed mall of comparable size. As a result, lease rates were higher, but even though the developer reports the region's retail market is saturated, the center is over 90 percent leased.

Photograph: Steve Crecilius

Already, the project has succeeded as a town center. Residents have already established new traditions at the project: More than 5,000 people took part in the inaugural lighting of the 32-foot living Christmas tree. Southlands Town Center has created a town center where none had existed before.

Many community gathering areas were included in the project, to make it a true town center where crowds can gather for events such as fireworks displays.

Photograph: Callison/Chris Eden

Photograph: Callison/Chris Eden

Photograph: Callison/Chris Eden

MAJOR TENANTS		
NAME	TYPE	GLA (SQ. FT.)
Colorado Cinema	Multiscreen theater	72,347
Sports Authority	Sports equipment & apparel	39,943
Barnes & Noble	Bookstore	27,053

Public spaces at Southlands Town Center include homey touches like fire pits, carillons, a clock tower and iconic lampposts.

Photograph: Callison/Chris Eden

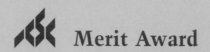

Sylvia Park

Auckland, New Zealand

Owner:
Kiwi Income Property Trust
Auckland, New Zealand

Management, Development and Leasing Company:
Kiwi Property Management Limited
Auckland, New Zealand

Design and Production Architects:
Jasmax
Auckland, New Zealand
NHA
Melbourne, Australia

Graphic Designers:
Jasmax
Auckland, New Zealand
NHA
Melbourne, Australia

Lighting Designer:
Connell Wagner
Auckland, New Zealand

Landscape Architect:
Isthmus
Auckland, New Zealand

General Contractor:
Brookfield Multiplex
Auckland, New Zealand

Gross size of center:
728,579 sq. ft.

**Gross leasable area
(small shop space, excluding anchors):**
368,576 sq. ft.

Total acreage of site:
60 acres

Type of center:
Regional

Physical description:
Two-level hybrid center

Location of trading area:
Suburban

Population:
- Primary trading area
  87,110
- Secondary trading area
  281,860
- Annualized percentage of shoppers
  anticipated to be from outside trade
  area: 5%

Development schedule:
- Opening date
  June 28, 2007

Parking spaces:
- 4,010

Sylvia Park in suburban Auckland is the largest shopping center in New Zealand—40 percent bigger than the next largest. Built on a former brownfield site, the project is the first stage of what will ultimately be a 2.5-million-square-foot town center containing commercial offices, residential units, community buildings and educational facilities. It is also one of the largest privately funded development projects in the nation's history.

Construction took nearly three years. Management felt that the market could absorb the opening of no more than 50 shops at any given time, so store debuts were broken into four stages from June 2006 to June 2007 allowing high-quality fit-outs and simultaneous trading of all stores in a given stage.

Given the center's size, four separate contractors received pieces of the project, with the largest engaged first to oversee comprehensive planning. One such effort

Sylvia Park brought in retailers that are both new to Auckland, giving shoppers greater diversity.

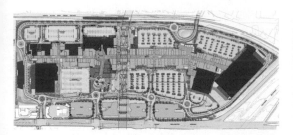

The staged open-ings of Sylvia Park allowed for 50 stores to debut at a time.

The use of vibrant color won an architectural award for color.

MAJOR TENANTS

NAME	TYPE	GLA (SQ. FT.)
The Warehouse	Discount department store	135,003
Hoyts 10	Multiscreen cinema	103,489
PAK'nSAVE	Supermarket	71,031
Foodtown	Supermarket	50,481

was to deal with the SEART Motorway. This four-lane highway cuts through the site and some construction took place beneath the highway, which was significant because the retailers under the roadway would form the critical connection between the mall's north and south sides. A public park under the motorway increases Sylvia Park's appeal to visitors.

The mall is arranged in linear fashion and is nearly one-half-mile long. There are distinct shopping precincts and several anchors, including two supermarkets. Retailers include 12 new to New Zealand and 40 new to Auckland and to the shopping center environment. Designers planned for an open-air retail lane, but the area's frequent rainfall prompted the addition of a tall glazed canopy with louvered natural ventilation, giving both a sense of the outdoors and protection from precipitation.

To encourage longer shopper stays in the massive project, planners included amenities: hotel-quality

The main malls are flooded with natural light during the day.

toilets, large and inviting parents' rooms, abundant mall seating, landscaping, water features, sculpture, open public spaces and directional signage. Cinemas, a bar, restaurants, two playgrounds, a child-care facility and a gymnasium provide leisure-time options. Extensive landscaping and use of vibrant colors further distinguish Sylvia Park from other retail destinations. The mall has won awards for its landscaping and use of architectural color.

The center must accommodate transportation in many ways, since nearly half of Auckland's population lives within a 20-minute drive and 186,000 cars pass the site each day. There are two decked parking structures; the first at the basement and ground levels, serving one of the supermarkets. The other is on the ground and first levels, connected to the mall's northern part by a covered walkway across the 15-foot road that separates the two. More parking is being added. Shoppers arriving by mass transit may arrive at the nation's first privately funded railway station or via a bus interchange. Within a year of its opening, the railway station had become one of the top 10 stops in Auckland for passenger volume.

While the project was 100 percent private investment on private land, the local government played a key role by supporting the site's rezoning from its former industrial purposes in return for the developer's use of best practices in site development. The Auckland City Council now promotes Sylvia Park as a model project for others to follow.

Unique designs, such as this entrance to the movie theater, can be found throughout the center.

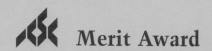

Urban Dock LaLaport Toyosu

Koto-ku, Tokyo, Japan

Owners:

Mitsui Fudosan Co., Ltd.
Tokyo, Japan

Ishikawayjima-Harima Heavy Industry Co., Ltd.
Tokyo, Japan

Management, Development and Leasing Company:
Mitsui Fudosan Co., Ltd.
Tokyo, Japan

Design Architect:
Laguarda.Low Architects
Dallas, Texas, United States

Production Architect:
Taisei Corporation
Tokyo, Japan

Graphic Designer:
RSM Design
San Clemente, California, United States

Lighting Designer:
Bliss-Fasman Lighting Design
New York, New York, United States

Landscape Architect:
Earthscape, Inc.
Tokyo, Japan

General Contractor:
Taisei Corporation
Beijing, China

Gross size of center:
1,184,040 sq. ft.

Gross leasable area (small shop space, excluding anchors):
204,224 sq. ft.

Total acreage of site:
16.67 acres

Type of center:
Superregional

Physical description:
Six-level mall

Location of trading area:
Urban but not central business district

Population:
- Primary trading area
  510,000
- Secondary trading area
  760,000
- Annualized percentage of shoppers anticipated to be from outside trade area: 5%

Development schedule:
- Opening date
  October 5, 2006

Parking spaces:
- 2,200

A ferry is one of several ways by which shoppers can reach Urban Dock LaLaport Toyosu on Tokyo Bay.

*L*ocated on the site of the historic IHI dockyards in the Tokyo Bay area, Urban Dock LaLaport Toyosu is a retail and lifestyle center that unites the historical significance of its location with a fresh perspective on the shopping experience.

The center contains 200 stores and a variety of dining and entertainment options. It is comprised of two buildings. The smaller—Parcel 4—is a two-level retail center with two levels of roof parking. The larger building—Parcel 6—is a three-level retail center highlighting four boat forms that suggest the variety of ships built on the site over the years. These boat forms make up an outdoor plaza from which shoppers have stunning views of the bay. This area also offers outdoor retail pavilions.

Access is a key issue for this waterfront center. The Toyosu project is the first shopping center to use a ferry to bring shoppers and tourists from other parts of Tokyo Bay. It also relies on mass-transit systems—ferry, subway, monorail and buses—to bring shoppers, who can also drive to the center by car.

One of the key design factors was how to maintain or restore the memory of the urban place, which holds historic status as a "municipal cultural and industrial urban asset" of the city of Tokyo. To achieve this, the design incorporated seawater and led to restoring an old crane as a visible symbol of the place.

The center is at the heart of the city of Tokyo, an appealing location for retired Japanese who return to live in the city.

MAJOR TENANTS

NAME	TYPE	GLA (SQ. FT.)
United Cinemas	Multiscreen cinema	777,777
KidZania Tokyo	Entertainment	66,666
Tokyu Hands	Department store	55,555
Do Sports Plaza	Health/fitness center	41,111
Food Store Aoki	Supermarket	30,000

Developers indicate that the Toyosu project is the first large-scale shopping center within Tokyo's 23 wards; other centers are on Tokyo's outskirts and require at least an hour's drive.

Consequently, the Toyosu project is favored by older Japanese, who tend to move back to the city center to ease their commute to work. The center's supermarkets, gymnasiums and multiscreen cinema further enhance the center's appeal to nearby residents, solidifying its role as both a lifestyle and retail destination.

*Even by the bay,
land use density
around Tokyo
required that the
mall rise to six
stories.*

*Designers took
every opportunity
(above) to share the
harbor views with
shoppers.*

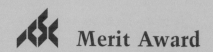

Merit Award

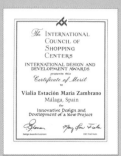

Vialia Estación María Zambrano

Málaga, Spain

Owner:
NECSA (Riofisa/ADIF)
Madrid, Spain

Management Company:
Jones Lang LaSalle
Madrid, Spain

Design Architects:
Riofisa
Madrid, Spain
RTKL Associates
London, United Kingdom

Production Architects:
Riofisa
Madrid, Spain
COOT
Madrid, Spain

Graphic Designer:
Fileni & Fileni
Buenos Aires, Argentina

Lighting Designers:
T. Kondos Associates
New York, New York, United States
Monlux
Madrid, Spain

Landscape Architect:
Riofisa
Madrid, Spain

General Contractor:
Eralan
Madrid, Spain

Development Company:
NECSA (Riofisa/ADIF)
Madrid, Spain

Leasing Company:
Riofisa
Madrid, Spain

Gross size of center:
151,739 sq. ft.

**Gross leasable area
(small shop space, excluding anchors):**
131,277 sq. ft.

Total acreage of site:
16.7 acres

Type of center:
Regional mixed use

Physical description:
Two-level enclosed mall

Location of trading area:
Urban central business district

Population:
- Primary trading area
552,290
- Secondary trading area
651,000
- Annualized percentage of shoppers anticipated to be from outside trade area: 15%

Development schedule:
- Opening date
November 27, 2006

Parking spaces:
- 1,300

Vialia Estación María Zambrano shopping center in Málaga, Spain, combines retailing with an established train station.

Vialia Estacíon María Zambrano is a mixed-use shopping and leisure center within a train station in Málaga, Spain, that receives many of the region's six million annual visitors. The center includes a transportation hub for buses and trains, over 20 restaurants, 105 retail shops and seven anchors, which include apparel stores, a multiscreen cinema with cutting-edge image and sound systems, a family playground and bowling alleys, a hotel and the train station itself.

The mall's design recognizes public fascination with trains and their movement. Many mall locations and the food court offer views of the trains from many levels. To build the new shopping center within the working train station, the contractor established 10 phases for the crews. First, they built the two-floor underground parking lot and raised the perimetral walls where high-speed train tracks would soon be laid. Next came the long pillarless canopy over the train platforms and refurbishment of the train station, followed by a temporary travel center and its access routes. Later, the retail areas atop the parking levels were added and the rail lines laid down. Finally, they built the hotel and enhanced the surroundings.

In laying out the mall, designers gave top priority to maximizing storefront visibility. Facades are large and units are placed so visitors pass by all stores. Signage, wall murals, balconies, broad casements, elevators and light all enhance the shopping experience.

MAJOR TENANTS

NAME	TYPE	GLA (SQ. FT.)
Hotel Barceló	Hotel	150,695
Lux Cinemas	Multiscreen theater	55,929
Media Markt	Electronics	44,000
RENFE	Railway	21,797
H&M	Apparel	21,130
Zara	Apparel	20,957
Sfera	Apparel	16,393

To build the retail area without affecting train operations, construction managers split the work into 10 phases.

Designers placed striking drop ceilings made of precast carton plaster panels in both the railway and retail malls. The panels also served as acoustic resonators. Using multiple surfaces overhead and tilting them in different directions helped reduce sound levels in the mall. The roof serves to unify the distinct activities taking place underneath its gentle slope.

Construction accommodated environmental concerns. Teams con-

trolled truck traffic and accesses, using schedules and itineraries to reduce inconveniencing railway passengers. Crews delivered waste to appropriate containers for recycling. Docking bays were located underground and in hidden spaces to minimize the visual impact of trucks.

The building was set back over 90 feet from a main boulevard to increase the green space around the mall. The area's frequent droughts prompted use of indigenous plants in outdoor areas and self-sufficient gardening indoors. A canopy at the front facade provides shade, reduc-

ing temperatures for arriving shoppers.

Natural cross ventilation helps reduce air-conditioning costs. Breaks in the roof were kept small and few to minimize hot daylight. Horizontal louvers manage sunlight at southern exposures. The impressive lighting display on the exterior facade was situated carefully in order to avoid disturbing adjacent residential buildings.

The developer recently added a Media Markt electronics anchor to the center, further enhancing the appeal of this mixed use project.

While visitors are usually focused on shopping opportunities (below), many locations such as the food court offer good views of arriving and departing trains.

Breaks in the roof (below and right) were few and small, to lessen the hot Málaga daylight.

Vioro

Fukuoka City, Japan

Owner:
Tokyo Tatemono Co., LTD
Tokyo, Japan

Management, Development and Leasing Company:
Tokyo Tatemono Co., LTD
Tokyo, Japan

Design Architects:
Laguarda.Low Architects
Dallas, Texas, United States
Laguarda.Low + Tanamachi
Tokyo, Japan
INA
Tokyo, Japan

Production Architect:
Takenaka Corporation
Tokyo, Japan

Graphic and Lighting Designer:
Nomura Kogei Ltd.
Tokyo, Japan

General Contractor:
Takenaka Corporation
Tokyo, Japan

Gross size of center:
119,759 sq. ft.

Gross leasable area
(small shop space, excluding anchors):
50,541 sq. ft.

Total acreage of site:
.38 acres

Type of center:
Fashion/specialty

Physical description:
11-level enclosed mall

Location of trading area:
Urban central business district

Population:
- Primary trading area
  300,000
- Secondary trading area
  1 million
- Annualized percentage of shoppers
  anticipated to be from outside trade
  area: 80%

Development schedule:
- Opening date
  October 2006

Parking spaces:
- Two for service dock only

Vioro in Fukuoka City, Japan, occupies a high-visibility corner on the city's high-end commercial street.

*V*ioro, in Japan's Fukuoka City, is a reinvention of the modern department store. It is only the second urban specialty center in the city and the first developed privately.

The center occupies a corner site at the busiest intersection of the city's high-end commercial street. Two levels below ground are linked to the subway and subterranean shopping passages.

The six levels above grade offer venues for hip young shoppers in the Tenjin area. There, the highly transparent retail units turn the typical department store inside out, reinterpreting normally blank facades into glass and high-graphic treatments. Large-scale boxes and folded planes overlap horizontal surfaces. Display light boxes at every level float within larger forms, drawing interest from shoppers on lower floors.

Apparel retailers dominate, but the center works to appeal to

Local retailers comprise 80 percent of tenants—a key factor in the center's success.

MAJOR TENANTS		
NAME	**TYPE**	**GLA (SQ. FT.)**
United Arrows	Fashion	6,700
Bar del Maestro	Restaurant	2,230

Designers used a range of textures— steel mesh, illuminated glass surfaces and patterned stones.

every consumer need of the young urban dweller—from an urban delicatessen to basic and casual clothing to health and beauty products. The rooftop dining terrace overlooks Fukuoka's commercial district.

Design influences almost every surface. Intricate steel meshes, patterned stones and illuminated glazed surfaces are generously used, adding variety to the dense retail floors.

The cost of land in the Fukuoka business district is extremely high, and the owner was able to develop a special urban-redevelop-ment allowance in conjunction with the city government. The owner offered leases to all tenants with rents based solely on percentage of sales. No fixed or base rent was allowed. Using this approach, the owner was able to attract 30 international retail brands for the center's opening.

Local brands account for 80 percent of the retailers, to which developers credit much of the project's success. This local flavor, tied to the clean visual lines of the architecture and interior design, has made Vioro a popular shopping spot for young urban dwellers.

The diagrams above show the center layout above and below ground.

High graphic treatments (right) are meant to appeal to the area's young shoppers.

Galerija Centrs

Riga, Latvia

Owner:
Linstow AS
Oslo, Norway

Management and Development Company:
Linstow Center Management Ltd.
Riga, Latvia

Design and Production Architects:
AMB International Architects & Designers, Ltd.
Riga, Latvia
Arplan Ltd.
Riga, Latvia

Graphic Designer:
AMB International Architects & Designers, Ltd.
Riga, Latvia

Lighting Designers:
AMB International Architects & Designers, Ltd.
Riga, Latvia
FLOS
Oslo, Norway

Landscape Architect:
Arplan Ltd.
Riga, Latvia

General Contractor:
SBRE Unlimited Liability Company
Riga, Latvia

Gross size of center:
- Before renovation/expansion
  154,419 sq. ft.
- After renovation/expansion
  321,678 sq. ft.

Current gross leasable area (small shop space, excluding anchors):
152,280 sq. ft.

Total acreage of site:
7.4 acres

Type of center:
Fashion/specialty

Physical description:
Seven-level enclosed mall

Location of trading area:
Urban central business district

Population:
- Primary trading area
  47,300
- Secondary trading area
  106,500
- Annualized percentage of shoppers anticipated to be from outside trade area: 10–15%

Development schedule:
- Opening date
  1938
- Renovation/expansion date
  August 2006

Parking spaces:
- None

Galerija Centrs rejuvenates a property that had been used for retail purposes for 70 years. Developers worked with state and UNESCO officials in preserving the site's historical qualities.

Finally, increasing competition in the market required more space than the old building allowed.

Renovation and expansion of the center had many positive effects. The design look of the site could become unified after eliminating the old uses of the property. By rebuilding and renovating the whole complex of buildings, the center modernized its technical and commercial logistics and waste management. The sense of newness helped reposition the center to show off its new upscale tenants, and the expansion gave Galerija Centrs more presence in the competitive market.

Today, Galerija Centrs is a contemporary fashion gallery with an ensemble of historic and new buildings surrounding a pedestrian street under a glass roof. Design components sought to create a 21st-century look within the heart of the old city: handrails, stairs and facades were chosen for this effect. The center retains old streetlight fixtures.

The historic nature of the district complicated the design and development process. The highest levels of city government and nongovernmental organizations were engaged at each stage of design and development. Developers consulted the State Inspection for Heritage Protection and, since old

The internal pedestrian street (below) includes planters and natural daylight.

Riga is on UNESCO's list of World Heritage sites, the international agency needed to be involved in the project as well.

In 2002, the center management and the Latvian Architect Union ran an open architectural competition for the best development proposal for the project. By 2005, the authorities approved technical designs for the center and issued the main building permit. Reconstruction began in January 2006, when 99 percent of the shops in the old center closed.

Due to its ground-floor location, only the grocery store remained open at the start of the renovation. By April, however, even the supermarket closed to finalize construction.

In August 2006, the renovated and expanded Galerija Centrs opened as a fashion gallery featuring several brand names new to the market: Marco Polo, Tommy Hilfiger, Alberto Fabiani, More&More, Diesel, GANT, Roxy/Quicksilver, Pierre Cardin, La Sense, Claire/Brubaker and others.

While historic imperatives affected exterior design, interiors (below) are clearly contemporary.

*Glass walls make
it easy for shoppers
to view apparel—
the retail heart of
Galerija Centrs.*

When the development process began in 1997, site sustainability, water and energy efficiency, material recyclability and reuse were not the major considerations they became in the next decade—nor wcrc landscaping and irrigation issues. Nonetheless, the developer is seeking environmental enhancements such as water-flow controllers on toilet-water taps that would decrease the taps' water consumption by 30 percent.

Galerija Centrs offers a shopping experience found nowhere else: On every floor, customers are brought in touch with the cobbled streets of old Riga, weaving the old with the new.

Kolona Spa offers a relaxing respite from shopping.

The enhanced floor treatments (below left) complement the window balconies of the existing exterior.

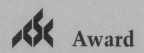
Stary Browar

Poznan, Poland

Owner and Development Company:
FORTIS "Nowy Stary Browar" LLC Partnership
Poznan, Poland

Management and Leasing Company:
FORTIS Centrum "50/50 Project" LLC Partnership
Poznan, Poland

Design and Production Architect:
Studio ADS Limited Liability Company
Poznan, Poland

Graphic Designer:
DIAGRAM
Poznan, Poland

Lighting Designer:
Studio ADS Limited Liability Company
Poznan, Poland

Landscape Architect:
Studio ADS Limited Liability Company
Poznan, Poland

General Contractor:
Hochtief Polska Limited Liability Company
Warsaw, Poland

Gross size of center:
- Before renovation/expansion
  256,873 sq. ft.
- After renovation/expansion
  529,826 sq. ft.

**Current gross leasable area
(small shop space, excluding anchors):**
258,703 sq. ft.

Total acreage of site:
28.4 acres

Type of center:
Superregional fashion/specialty

Physical description:
Seven-level enclosed mall

Location of trading area:
Urban central business district

Population:
- Primary trading area
  797,900
- Secondary trading area
  3.4 million
- Annualized percentage of shoppers
  anticipated to be from outside trade
  area: 7%

Development schedule:
- Opening date
  November 5, 2003
- Renovation/expansion date
  March 11, 2007

Parking spaces:
- 1,055

*Stary Browar in
Poznan, Poland, was
built on the site of an
old brewery, putting
several of the old
edifices to new use.*

Stary browar means "old brewery," and visitors to the shopping center of that name in Poznan, Poland, can still spend time in the 19th-century former malt house, kettle house, kiln house and the brewer's administration buildings. Each has been carefully refurbished and transformed into retail settings in the project's renovation and expansion.

Today Stary Browar's seven buildings host 208 shops, cafes, restaurants and an eight-screen cinema. They also contain professional studios, a concert hall, an art gallery and a high-concept hotel. Plans call for a 10-acre park to cover an underground museum of contemporary art.

The largest building is the seven-story Atrium, with four retail floors, plus two office floors shared with parking on three levels, including the roof. Another major building, the Passage, holds three

The new building offers seven levels of activity, including an eight-screen cinema.

Photographs on this page: Robert Mendel

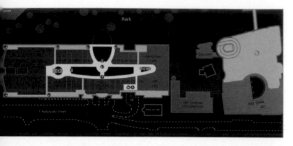

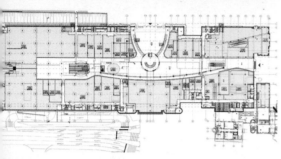

MAJOR TENANTS		
NAME	**TYPE**	**GLA (SQ. FT.)**
van Graaf	Fashion	33,887
Mega Avans	Electronics	32,775
Multikino	Multiscreen cinema	31,956
Piotr I Pawel	Delicatessen	30,537

The site plan shows the interrelationships of the various buildings in the Stary Browar complex.

The 19th century brewery's structures (below) were restored over several years. Visitors can now pass hours in the former malt house, kettle house and kiln house.

Photograph: Maciej Kuszela

Architectural and engineering experts have lauded Stary Browar's integration of the old buildings and new.

Photograph: Maciej Kuszela

retail levels and three levels of underground parking. The Pólwiejska 32 mixed-use building contains a three-level H&M store and four levels of offices. Blow-Up Hall, a former military court, has been converted into a concept hotel.

The center's development was done in phases. The owner acquired the deteriorating brewery buildings and site in 1998. Three years of planning were followed by construction and the late 2003 opening of the first section: the Atrium. The popular space soon had no retail vacancies and boasted visits of over nine million people per year. With the project's success and opening of two competitive centers nearby, plans moved forward for the opening of the expansion (the Passage) in March 2007.

After the retail-focused Atrium opened, the owner imagined the Passage as having more leisure and entertainment functions than the Atrium. The owner conducted a survey that asked customers which retail brands were under-represented in the first section. The results led to a tenant mix for the new section dominated by

Photograph: Maciej Szarejko

upscale fashion brands such as MaxMara, Patrizia Pepé, Laurel, Schumacher, Liu-Jo, Anna RitaN, Baldinini, Bugatti and Diesel—all grouped on one floor. The expansion also included a multiscreen cinema and home design and sports/leisure retailers. In 2009, Stary Browar introduced newcomer Zara Home to Poland and to the Poznan market, Pollini, Versace Jeans, COCCINELLE, Max&Co, Lacoste and Stradivarius. Finally, the museum

The iconic clock tower (above) is the most recognizable symbol at the old brewery. The new building (top) stretches into the distance.

Photography: Maciej Kuszela

Photograph: Maciej Kuszela

Photograph: Archive of Stary Browar

Photograph: Agnieszka Szenrok

of contemporary art completes the owner's idea of transforming abandoned buildings into the vibrant central district of Poznan.

The owner believed that the center's design should be based equally on retail priorities as well as artistic content. It is a great concept of 50 percent business and 50 percent art. The center's buildings each reflect that concept. The Passage, the Atrium, the Courtyard of Art and others contain works of art. The center cooperates with culture promoting and charity organizations and institutions such as the Children's Artistic Centre, the Malta Theatre Festival and the Great Orchestra of Christmas Charity.

Construction of the expansion did not affect operation of the Atrium's stores, but access to parking levels, unloading ramps and the Courtyard of Art was hindered somewhat. To minimize the impact of construction, the most troublesome work was done at

A Courtyard of Art in the old buildings grew from the developer's concept that the center's design should be balanced between business and art.

The developer is interested in using the Courtyard of Art as a means to work with nonprofit cultural institutions.

Photograph: Jacek Bakutis

Photograph: Robert Mendel

Visitors can peer outward to see mature trees, carefully preserved in the restoration.

Photograph: Maciej Kuszela

Photograph: Robert Mendel

Photograph: Jacek Bakutis

Photograph: Rafal Kupczyk

night. Clearly marked separate access roads for customers and construction crews were opened and security staff directed traffic.

Stary Browar's expansion spent no public monies. Further, the developer was required to modernize the roads next to the center. Work on Kosciuszki Street—the main access road—jammed roads to the center and caused long delays in exiting from the parking levels. To reduce this impact, the developer temporarily suspended parking fees, waiting drivers received refreshments and retailers could distribute free parking vouchers to their customers. Construction brought no drop in shopper counts, but use of parking lots fell 30 percent during the expansion period.

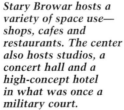

Stary Browar hosts a variety of space use—shops, cafes and restaurants. The center also hosts studios, a concert hall and a high-concept hotel in what was once a military court.

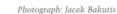

Photograph: Jacek Bakutis

*A huge checkerboard
in the mall area lends
a touch of playfulness
to the multi-dimen-
sional Stary Browar.*

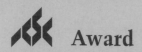

Westfield San Francisco Centre

San Francisco, California, United States

Owner and Development Company:
Forest City Enterprises/Westfield, LLC
Los Angeles, California, United States

Management and Leasing Company:
Westfield, LLC
Los Angeles, California, United States

Design Architects:
RTKL Associates Inc.
Los Angeles, California, United States
Westfield Design
Los Angeles, California, United States
Kohn Pedersen Fox
New York, New York, United States

Production Architect:
ka Architecture
Cleveland, Ohio, United States

Graphic Designer:
Communications Arts, Inc.
Boulder, Colorado, United States

Lighting Designer:
Horton Lees Brogden Lighting Design
San Francisco, California, United States

Landscape Architect:
Land Design
Pomona, California, United States

General Contractor:
Westfield Corporation, Inc.
Los Angeles, California, United States
Forest City Commercial California
Los Angeles, California, United States

Gross size of center:
- Before renovation/expansion
  498,216 sq. ft.
- After renovation/expansion
  1,212,688 sq. ft.

**Current gross leasable area
(small shop space, excluding anchors):**
446,856 sq. ft.

Total acreage of site:
6.36 acres

Type of center:
Mixed-use regional

Physical description:
High-rise atrium

Location of trading area:
Urban central business district

Population:
- Primary trading area
  2.6 million
- Annualized percentage of shoppers
  anticipated to be from outside trade
  area: 50%

Development schedule:
- Opening date
  Fall 1988
- Renovation/expansion date
  September 2006

Parking spaces:
- None

A historic department store was merged with an existing regional mall to create the new Westfield San Francisco Centre.

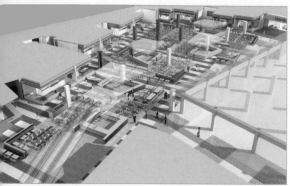

Illustration: RTKL Associates, Inc.

MAJOR TENANTS		
NAME	**TYPE**	**GLA (SQ. FT.)**
Bloomingdale's	Department store	352,416
Nordstrom	Department store	312,000
Century Theatres	Multiscreen cinema	52,636
Bristol Farms	Market	28,780
Borders	Bookstore	20,000

*(Top left) This illustration shows the layout of the foodcourt.
(Bottom left) The Art Deco dome of the historic Emporium department store can be seen near the top center.*

An early plan to make a flagship Bloomingdale's store in the old Emporium space was abandoned due to seismic regulations. Instead, a new edifice holds the Bloomingdale's anchor.

Photograph: © RTKL/David Whitcomb

*T*he renovation and expansion of the Westfield San Francisco Centre merged the existing Westfield Centre with adjacent space once occupied by the Emporium department store, which was designed in 1896. The Emporium's survival of the 1906 earthquake caused locals to hail it as a "symbol of fortitude and hope."

The Emporium building, however, had fallen into disrepair after the store's closing in 1995. It comprised about 650,000 square feet in three buildings: the old store, an office annex and an old warehouse structure, each facing a different street. Initially, the owner sought to renovate the Emporium as a flagship Bloomingdale's department store, but seismic and other improvements needed to comply with current code requirements made that plan unfeasible.

Eventually, the developers created a plan that would preserve and restore historic elements of the

building while allowing modern construction to meet the requirements of the new Bloomingdale's. Later, the plan was modified to allow the restored building to integrate seamlessly with the existing Westfield retail complex.

The resulting center contains two department stores—the new Bloomingdale's and the Westfield's Nordstrom—as well as 172 specialty shops, many of which are new to the United States market. It also has a nine-screen cinema, a gourmet food market, international and local restaurants and casual dining.

The center's design incorporates the Emporium's historic architecture, including its restored Beaux Arts facade and signature dome. The dome was raised 54 feet and suspended onto a new foundation. Nearly a year of planning was required to raise the 250-ton dome, which drew international attention as an engineering feat. Abundant natural light now

streams through the restored crown and lunette windows, which illuminate the atrium. The design of each floor reflects a different aspect of San Francisco life. Escalators and stairwells include the original Art Deco-era balustrades, stairs and treads. The dome and facade are painted in colors reminiscent of those used in San Francisco in the early 1900s.

The high-rise retail structure (top left) holds 172 stores, a nine-screen cinema and many options for upscale and casual dining. The center (above) is readily accessible from the streets of San Francisco.

Photograph: © Tim Griffith

A glass roof offers natural illumination of the immense space.

There are two grand entrances to the complex. On the north, the Market Street entrance showcases the restored historic facade. On the south, the Mission Street entrance features Bloomingdale's modern "jewel-box" design that allows passersby to view activity within. The building's "tilted-box" design creates a corridor between the two entrances that acts as a gateway from the nearby cultural/convention area to other commercial venues.

Several nonarchitectural factors contribute to the project's success. In addition to the corridor connecting to other venues, the center is within easy walking distance of several major hotels and residential towers. It sits at a major junction of several modes of public transportation: the BART

Photograph: © Tim Griffith

The old Emporium store withstood the 1906 earthquake and now displays banners trumpeting the center, the anchors and the cinema.

Courtesy of Westfield

The gourmet food court (left) is often filled with upscale shoppers.

Photograph: © RTKL/David Whitcomb

Raising the old Emporium's 250-ton dome (below) by 54 feet took nearly a year of planning.

subway station, the Muni Metro Light Rail Subway Line and the Powell Street cable car station are all adjacent to the center. An at-grade trolley, an extensive municipal bus service and a large public parking garage are nearby.

Internally, the two buildings are linked on five levels. The restored rotunda serves as a connector between the first floor of Nordstrom and the top floor of Bloomingdale's.

Several measures aided shopper safety and traffic during construction. Exterior screening of the construction site protected shoppers from falling debris, braced the Market Street facade during renovation and mitigated dust and other airborne pollutants. One adjacent street was closed periodically to shield shoppers from injury during demolition and construction. Barricades and existing double fire doors in the Westfield center kept shoppers away from construction sites while wall openings, mall connections and reconfigured tenant spaces were built to tie the two buildings together.

Photograph: © Tim Griffith

The developers needed to work with stringent water, energy, waste and atmospheric environmental restrictions in creating the center. Further, a ban on new on-site parking caused the inclusion of bicycle storage, locker room and shower facilities at the center. After a decade-long development process costing nearly $500 million, the developers and city have created a world-class economic, historic and social venue.

Photograph: © RTKL/David Whitcomb

Open storefronts throughout the Westfield San Francisco Centre create easier access for shoppers.

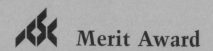

Merit Award

Renovation or Expansion of an Existing Project

Alstertal-Einkaufszentrum Hamburg

Hamburg, Germany

Owner:

Klosterstern KG
Hamburg, Germany

Management, Development and Leasing Company:

ECE Projektmanagement GmbH & Co. KG
Hamburg, Germany

Design Architect:

ECE Projektmanagement GmbH & Co. KG
Hamburg, Germany

Production and Landscape Architect:

Architekturbüro Knud Jensen
Hamburg, Germany

Graphic Designer:

ECE Projektmanagement GmbH & Co. KG
Hamburg, Germany

Lighting Designers:

Michael Batz
Hamburg, Germany

Lichtplanung Peter Andres
Hamburg, Germany

General Contractor:

ECE Projektmanagement GmbH & Co.KG
Hamburg, Germany

Gross size of center:
- Before renovation/expansion
  673,627 sq. ft.
- After renovation/expansion
  1,062,161 sq. ft.

Current gross leasable area (small shop space, excluding anchors):
465,861 sq. ft.

Total acreage of site:
24.4 acres

Type of center:
Superregional lifestyle

Physical description:
Five-level enclosed mall

Location of trading area:
Suburban

Population:
- Primary trading area
  54,000
- Secondary trading area
  753,000
- Annualized percentage of shoppers anticipated to be from outside trade area: 15%

Development schedule:
- Opening date
  November 1970
- Renovation/expansion date
  September 2006

Parking spaces:
- 3,000

*B*uilt in 1970, Alstertal-Einkaufszentrum Hamburg (AEZ) was the largest suburban shopping center in the Hamburg market. With its expansion in 2006, it has become the largest shopping center in northern Germany, offering 241 shops.

The expansion brought more than added retail. The developers attribute the project's success to the coherency of the overall concept. The "shopping of a very special kind" concept encompassed the renovation of not just the center but the redesign of the entire urban surroundings. A new urban quarter was created with new facilities such as a post office, a bank, public authorities, physician offices and a fitness center.

Access also played a key role in the expansion's success. Close to two freeways, the center offers 3,000 parking spaces. A city railway station is adjacent to the center, bringing shoppers from the central city to AEZ in 20 minutes. A bus station serving seven bus lines is at the center's front door, and many bicycle stands are in front of the center.

Leasing to locals was another integral component of the center's success: A large proportion of retailers are from Hamburg and its environs. National and international brands also populate the center. The renovated center includes expanded space for existing tenants and a tenant mix that includes a new focus on youth retailers.

Expansion of Alstertal-Einkaufszentrum Hamburg made the city's largest mall into the biggest shopping center in northern Germany.

Careful planning kept stores open by day and evening as construction progressed.

MAJOR TENANTS		
NAME	TYPE	GLA (SQ. FT.)
P&C	Apparel	68,846
H&M	Apparel	34,262
Rewe	Supermarket/Hypermarket	29,009
Appelrath-Cüpper	Apparel	27,114
Anson's	Apparel	23,756
C&A	Apparel	22,432
Thalia	Bookstore	20,721
Zara	Apparel	20,085

Efficient lighting practices include use of natural illumination from the glass roof over the mall area.

Shoppers and visitors were kept informed of construction progress with slogans such as "We're good already but getting even better" and "Today for Hamburg and the region—tomorrow for all of Northern Germany!" The center held press conferences and celebrations. Construction site festivities included the laying of the foundation stone and a topping-out ceremony. To reduce the visual clutter of the construction site, owners installed a professionally designed fence displaying announcements about new tenants.

The Emilia pizza and pasta restaurant is one of many dining options at Alstertal-Einkaufszentrum Hamburg.

The center's strong apparel focus is readily seen in many stores.

Many of the center's 3,000 parking spaces (top) are located on the roof.

Protected passageways were built featuring greenery and virtual illustrations of the new AEZ. The new "Infopoint" section offered visitors news about progress, new retailers and other aspects of the expansion and renovation.

Advertising buys ranged from TV and radio spots to baggage conveyor belts. Group-specific marketing events included open-air classical music concerts on the upper parking deck, a fashion event with winners of a TV talent show, a children's holiday program and the Kulinarium—visual merchandising of the center's grocery businesses.

Planning gave high priority to resource conservation and environmental protection. Greenery appears around the square and along the streets. A green-roof area was installed, along with a biotope irrigation system that

recycles rainwater. Plants now vegetate large surfaces on the center's facade. Only natural plants are used for interior greenery.

To reduce energy consumption, the center uses more efficient lighting equipment, electronic upstream devices and a day/night control system. The operation time of escalators, the power level of the ventilators and illumination periods have all been reduced from pre-expansion practices. Over 80

percent of construction materials are recyclable, including concrete, steel, glass, the glass-barreled roof, aluminum, facade elements, natural stone used in facades and flooring and stone wool for insulation.

Through smart planning, the center did not need to close shops for a single day during the renovation and expansion and a vibrant new center was brought to the Hamburg market.

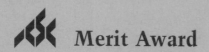

QueensPlaza

Brisbane, Australia

Owner:
CFS Retail Property Trust
Sydney, New South Wales, Australia

Management, Development and Leasing Company:
Colonial First State Property Management
Melbourne, Victoria, Australia

Design Architect:
RTKL Associates Inc.
Los Angeles, California, United States

Production Architect:
PDT Architects
Brisbane, Queensland, Australia

Graphic Designer:
Mim Design
Melbourne, Victoria, Australia

Lighting Designer:
DMA Professional Engineers
Melbourne, Victoria, Australia

General Contractor:
Watpac Construction Pty Ltd.
Brisbane, Queensland, Australia

Gross size of center:
- After renovation/expansion
  419,792 sq. ft.

Current gross leasable area (small shop space, excluding anchors):
115,500 sq. ft.

Total acreage of site:
2.1 acres

Type of center:
Central business district center

Physical description:
Five-level enclosed mall

Location of trading area:
Urban central business district

Population:
- Primary trading area
  78,891
- Secondary trading area
  133,545
- Annualized percentage of shoppers anticipated to be from outside trade area: 15%

Development schedule:
- Renovation/expansion opening dates
  Phase 1: June 2005
  Phase 2: December 2006
  Phase 3: November 2007

Parking spaces:
- 595

QueensPlaza in downtown Brisbane, Australia, brought high-end fashion retailing to that market, where fashionistas had previously traveled south to Sydney or Melbourne to shop.

The developer demolished seven buildings on three street frontages to make way for the five-level retail center, which sits atop five levels of underground parking. The site anchors two major street corners. The center's corners rake outwards, increasing its visibility.

The facade comprises glass and sandstone juxtaposed with contemporary sunshades. Upper levels incorporate wraparound balconies and window displays. Transparent ground-floor retail spaces attract shoppers from adjacent streets. The center's interior features soaring ceilings, distinctive finishes, column-free spaces and recessed lighting appropriate to the high-end retailers inside. Designers kept sight lines as clear as possible to enhance the sense of uncluttered space.

Australia's native pearls inspired the pure white look of QueensPlaza. Vertical glass panels introduce natural light to the center wherever possible. Contemporary touches such as black granite and polished concrete panels set in chamfers give dramatic definition to the white space. The center also offers the nation's first use of channel glass.

QueensPlaza's interior has been designed with a simple grid structure. Lightweight and flexible wall

New entrances (above and right) to QueensPlaza in Brisbane, Australia, are contrasted with a pre-renovation entryway (below).

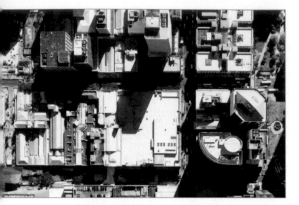

MAJOR TENANTS

NAME	TYPE	GLA (SQ. FT.)
David Jones	Department store	286,871
Coles	Supermarket	17,427
Decjuba	Specialty	2,153
Louis Vuitton	Specialty	2,196

Australia's native pearls inspired the center's design—highly polished white surfaces abound—and a 52-foot-wide dome is lined with mother-of-pearl shell, providing a striking accent to the design of QueensPlaza.

structures allow tenant spaces to change, expand and contract with relative ease and without much impact on the layout, ambience and design of the overall center. A David Jones flagship department store anchors the center, which offers 79 specialty stores.

A 52-foot-wide dome clad with mother-of-pearl shell tops QueensPlaza's major atrium. Columns within the mall are wrapped in polished, white, crystallized glass slabs. The lower two floors are sheeted externally in sandstone, while the upper three levels are tiled in reconstituted stone. The mall's signature circular pattern was created with water-laser technology. The 17-foot-high glazed-panel elevator doors at the Queen Street

entrance require three tons of counterweight to operate. The iconic original David Jones elevator was restored and now also serves the office floors above the retail levels.

QueensPlaza was the largest retail construction project in downtown Brisbane in two decades. Development stretched over five years, during which time the existing David Jones department store had to remain operational.

After demolition of the older buildings on the site, the project's first stage opened in June 2005, phase two in December 2006 and phase three in November 2007. By the time of the second-stage opening, the center was 100 percent leased with what the developer calls a "who's who" of international and national haute couture retailers as well as supermarket and food court units.

The center's branding campaign spoke about "The New Royalty"—the upscale shoppers who would be drawn to this new fashion center in downtown Brisbane. "Get some carrots with your carats" was used for the supermarket opening and "Simply delectable $5 fashion tips" promoted the food court.

Luxury shopping needs are met in posh surroundings at QueensPlaza.

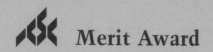
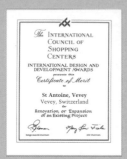

St Antoine, Vevey
Vevey, Switzerland

Owner:
Maus Frères SA
Geneva, Switzerland

Development and Leasing Company:
Maus Frères SA
Geneva, Switzerland

Design Architect:
Haskoll
London, United Kingdom

Production and Landscape Architect:
Richter et Dahl Rocha
Lausanne, Switzerland

Graphic and Lighting Designer:
Haskoll
London, United Kingdom

General Contractor:
Maus Frères SA
Geneva, Switzerland

Gross size of center:
- Before renovation/expansion
  21,571 sq. ft.
- After renovation/expansion
  24,940 sq. ft.

Total acreage of site:
6.7 acres

Type of center:
Regional

Physical description:
Four-level enclosed center

Location of trading area:
Urban but not central business district

Population:
- Primary trading area
  180,000
- Secondary trading area
  50,000

Development schedule:
- Opening date
  April 1973
- Renovation/expansion date
  April 2006

Parking spaces:
- 289

The 35-year-old St Antoine, Vevey in Switzerland had a complicated customer flow, which was improved by the renovation and expansion. A diagram (upper right) shows the center wrapped around a triangular atrium.

*T*he building that now holds the St Antoine Centre in Vevey, Switzerland, housed two department stores when it opened in 1973. With the closing of one store a decade later, the space became a shopping center with retail units surrounding an atrium anchored by the remaining department store. The center, clad in steel, was inward looking, with a pedestrian street located behind the street facade. The reconfigured center suffered from complex customer flow.

The new St Antoine Centre grew from the willingness of local authorities to narrow the adjacent main street, which allowed the new center to expand, have a new facade and face a new pedestrian walkway at ground level. Now, active frontages and shops at street level bring more shoppers into the mall.

Developers and designers sought to simplify and improve the design of the horizontal and vertical elements of the four-story

Lighted signage add to the ambiance at St Antoine, Vevey.

The riverside center (left) remained open throughout the renovation. Passersby (below) can now access the center through shops facing the street.

mall, which contains two additional levels of underground parking. The new design would promote better shopper flow, higher shop fronts and uncluttered sight lines. A dramatic new mall entrance leads to a new street entrance. New shops balance the former retail mix.

A restaurant on the mall's top level moved and expanded, its terrace enlarged to promote vertical circulation. Designers added a mall cafe at the lower ground level to enhance the shopping experience and reinforce pedestrian flow. Shopper traffic improved with new elevators and an underground garage.

The center remained open throughout its refurbishment. The expansion was built as a single unit, allowing existing shops to remain reasonably undisturbed. Some new retail spaces were completed earlier than others, letting some stores shift to new locations rather than close when their old space would be affected by construction. Much of the work in public spaces was done at night to avoid inconveniencing shoppers.

Inside, the mall's atrium displays a modern-art installation—a sculpture—that sits under the glass roof. Natural light from the roof reflects off the sculpture's 300 metal bars onto every nearby surface. Outside, a public open space overlooks a river. The space has been appropriately landscaped and provides a respite from the urban setting.

Environmental considerations included monitoring new targets for energy and water use by using

(Right) The highly polished white surfaces gives a ultra modern look to the center.

energy-efficient equipment. New light fixtures replaced old ones, further saving energy. A new heating and ventilation plant meets energy specifications. Paper, plastic, glass, batteries and tin are all separated and recycled.

The center's renovation also accommodated expansion of the long-standing department store, bringing new shoppers to the anchor and the 49 specialty stores in St Antoine Centre.

A glass ceiling (below) adds natural light to the center, while large display windows (right) exhibit merchandise to prospective shoppers.

MAJOR TENANTS		
NAME	**TYPE**	**GLA (SQ. FT.)**
Manor	Supermarket	25,532
Manora	Restaurant	10,086
Fust SA	Electrical	75,347
Ochsner Shoes	Sports	4,090

Reconfiguration of store entrances has re-energized traffic flow at St Antoine, Vevey.

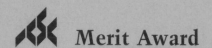

The Village at Fashion Fair

Fresno, California, United States

Owner:
Macerich
Santa Monica, California, United States

Management, Development and Leasing Company:
Macerich
Santa Monica, California, United States

Design and Production Architect:
F+A Architects
Pasadena, California, United States

Graphic Designer:
Scott | AG
Santa Rosa, California, United States

Lighting Designer:
Lighting Design Alliance
Signal Hill, California, United States

Landscape Architect:
Lynn Capouya, Inc.
Costa Mesa, California, United States

General Contractor:
The Whiting-Turner Contracting Company
Folsom, California, United States

Gross size of center:
- Before renovation/expansion 874,058 sq. ft.
- After renovation/expansion 956,122 sq. ft.

Current gross leasable area (small shop space, excluding anchors):
395,241 sq. ft.

Total acreage of site:
68.3 acres

Type of center:
Superregional

Physical description:
One-level open-air expansion

Location of trading area:
Suburban

Population:
- Primary trading area 602,041
- Secondary trading area 303,044
- Annualized percentage of shoppers anticipated to be from outside trade area: 17%

Development schedule:
- Opening date November 1970
- Renovation/expansion date December 5, 2005

Parking spaces:
- 4,559

The Village at Fashion Fair brought many new retailers to the Fresno market, including Sephora.

The Village at Fashion Fair is an open-air, lifestyle expansion of the existing Fashion Fair shopping center, which opened in 1970 and was redesigned and renovated in 2003. It was created specifically to respond to the market's need for high-quality lifestyle retailers and sit-down restaurants.

The Village plaza is well placed between the mall entrance and a heavily trafficked avenue. It contains four new structures. Two are freestanding restaurants (The Cheesecake Factory and Flemings Prime Steakhouse & Wine Bar); both offering terrace seating on large patios overlooking an open-air courtyard and a traditional-looking brick roadway. The other two buildings flank a courtyard and contain a combined 72,000 square feet of retail space and 19 new-to-market retailers including Anthropologie, BCBG MAX AZRIA, bebe and Sephora.

The Village architecture is adaptable to different styles and materials for each store space, resulting in a "village" of buildings that look as though they were built over time. Landscaping, ornamental and interactive fountains, benches and cafe seating offer shoppers a place to rest and refresh before continuing their visit. Developers say the average shopping visit at Fashion Fair mall is now almost 25 percent longer than the industry average. The adjacent mall entrance was expanded and enhanced for greater visibility.

MAJOR TENANTS		
NAME	TYPE	GLA (SQ. FT.)
Macy's	Department store	176,410
JCPenney	Department store	153,769
Gottschalks	Department store	154,052

The Village is an open-air lifestyle expansion to the existing Fashion Fair mall, which opened in 1970.

The two restaurant anchors offer terrace seating on patios (left).

The visual centerpiece of The Village is an interactive pop-jet fountain surrounded by a soft-surface deck. Misters in the plaza's trees refresh visitors during daytime temperatures that sometimes exceed 110 degrees. At night, Tivoli-style lights and the fountains' babbling waters create a warm and romantic atmosphere.

Other amenities enhanced the Village's focus on the family. Ample restrooms are complemented by a spacious family restroom area that includes a private nursing area and diaper-changing stations. The center includes state-of-the-art security equipment, and security guards undergo training to improve their sensitivity to families' concerns. When parking proved to be a problem during the holiday season, the developer had employees park at a satellite location and bused to stores, freeing up 2,000 parking spaces for shoppers.

Representatives from The Cheesecake Factory (a sought-after unit) were educated about Fresno via helicopter tours. The Cheesecake Factory served as a catalyst for many other upscale retailers to join the mix. To accommodate retailers still under construction during the phased opening, construction barricades displayed graphics of the coming-soon retailer brands.

With the holiday season soon following the opening, the marketing staff chose community musical groups as the focus of opening festivities. Shoppers enjoyed performances from school choirs, marching bands, jazz ensembles, chamber music groups and individual musicians. The events raised over $20,000 for local school music programs.
The remaining retailers opened in early July the following year and ceremonies included fireworks display with synchronized music

and a concert featuring a finalist from the *American Idol* TV series.

The project required flexible scheduling. While a good working relationship with the city of Fresno sped project approval within 62 days, the early part of the construction period was slowed by 29 consecutive days of rain during the Fresno valley's notorious wet season. Nonetheless, The Village at Fashion Fair attracted new shoppers, who on average spend more time at the center with these new retail offerings.

The open-air courtyard offers tree-shaded seating for visitors.

The Village at Fashion Fair offers many family-friendly options, including this play area, a family restroom and a nursing area.

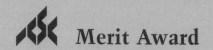

Merit Award

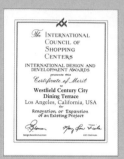

Westfield Century City Dining Terrace

Los Angeles, California, United States

Owner:
Westfield, LLC
Los Angeles, California, United States

Management, Development and Leasing Company:
Westfield, LLC
Los Angeles, California, United States

Design Architects:
Westfield Design with Corsini Stark Architects, Serrurier Architects, Atlaschi Architects, Young Lee, Akar Studio
Los Angeles, California, United States

Production Architect:
Rios Clementi Hale Studios
Los Angeles, California, United States

Graphic Designer:
RTKL Associates Inc.
Los Angeles, California, United States

Lighting Designer:
Frances Krahne & Associates
Los Angeles, California, United States

Landscape Architect:
Rios Clementi Hale Studios
Los Angeles, California, United States

General Contractor:
Westfield, LLC
Los Angeles, California, United States

Gross size of center:
- Before renovation/expansion
  20,200 sq. ft.
- After renovation/expansion
  30,000 sq. ft.

**Current gross leasable area
(small shop space, excluding anchors):**
30,000 sq. ft.

Total acreage of site:
.7 acres

Type of center:
Food court

Physical description:
Food court with interior and exterior seating

Location of trading area:
Urban central business district

Population:
- Primary trading area
  1,117,403
- Annualized percentage of shoppers anticipated to be from outside trade area: 40%

Development schedule:
- Renovation/expansion date
  December 15, 2005

Parking spaces:
- 2,490

The Dining Terrace at Westfield Century City provides office workers, hotel guests and shoppers with an upscale spot to congregate.

*T*he Dining Terrace at Westfield Century City in Los Angeles was developed to appeal to the employees of nearby office buildings, guests at adjacent luxury hotels and affluent customers drawn by the mall's new upscale retail tenants and the mall's entertainment sector with its multiplex cinema. To do so, designers and the developer created a new food court: a courtyard of modern teak furniture and floating planters containing sculptural greenery, exhibition cooking demonstrations and an indoor/outdoor ambience. The new food court was inspired by the dining terrace recently opened at another of the owner's properties in Sydney, Australia.

The local health department required enclosed tenancies, but the center knew that alfresco dining would attract customers, so designers created an indoor/ outdoor feel with wood and steel canopies and flamed-granite paving flowing through low iron butt-glazed glass. This visually extended the outdoor courtyard to a skylighted, restaurant-like space containing exhibition kitchens. The interior dining space features steel-trowel plaster walls and a clean white museum-quality ceiling. Its muted palette allows full expression for tenant design.

The developers knew the look and quality of tenants could be a drawing card, so it avoided standard prototype designs by providing seed money to hire local restaurant designers to create crisp modern designs using upscale materials. Menu boards and typical fast-

MAJOR TENANTS

NAME	TYPE	GLA (SQ. FT.)
Coral Tree Café	Food	959
Panda Express	Food	836
Italia Express	Food	836
Baja Fresh	Food	734
California Crisp	Food	730

Designers placed the new dining terrace on the Westfield Century City's southwest side, previously the least active part of the property.

food counters were not allowed. Instead, kitchen consultants promoted exhibition kitchens and sophisticated food displays.

Interior and exterior spaces are broken up by tenant islands with integrated counter seating, planters and other seating elements. Rich woods, soft-green resins, subdued stainless-steel signage and hidden light sources lend warmth to the space. The

Local restaurant designers brought new approaches to seating and service in the food court, adding exhibition kitchens and counter seating.

owner provides custom-designed china, glassware and cutlery to all tenants.

Seating remains communal, although traditional restaurant seating has been inserted along the periphery of the dining terraces. The restaurants include Lawry's Carvery, Sorabol Korean BBQ & Asian Noodles, Tacone Flavor Grill, Seiki-Shi Sushi, California Crisp and Coral Tree Express.

Designers placed the dining terrace on the mall site's southwest side, which had been the least active on the property, located a block off a main thoroughfare. The dining terrace's opening

Wood and steel canopies give an "indoor-outdoor" feeling to the Westfield Century City Dining Terrace.

became part of a Hollywood premiere night for the film *The Producers.* Celebrities' attendance created buzz for the new food court in the local, national and international media.

During the phased construction, the owner kept the old food court open on the opposite side of the mall property. With the opening of the new dining terrace, the old food court was closed to avoid competition and to draw hungry visitors to the new site. The opening of the new court was complemented with other new customer services such as concierge services and valet parking.

Sales figures at Westfield Century City's new dining terrace more than doubled those in the old location, showing that an upscale atmosphere can bring new life to a proven concept.

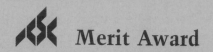
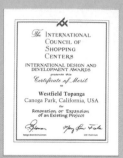

Westfield Topanga
Canoga Park, California, United States

Owner:
Westfield, LLC
Los Angeles, California, United States

Management, Development and Leasing Company:
Westfield, LLC
Los Angeles, California, United States

Design and Production Architect:
Westfield Design
Los Angeles, California, United States

Graphic Designer:
Sussman Prejza
Culver City, California, United States

Lighting Designer:
Horton Lees Brogden Lighting Design
Culver City, California, United States

Landscape Architect:
Rios Clementi Hale Studios
Los Angeles, California, United States

General Contractor:
Westfield, LLC
Los Angeles, California, United States

Gross size of center:
- Before renovation/expansion
  1,049,000 sq. ft.
- After renovation/expansion
  1,430,000 sq. ft.

**Current gross leasable area
(small shop space, excluding anchors):**
540,000 sq. ft.

Total acreage of site:
48.3 acres

Type of center:
Superregional

Physical description:
Two-level enclosed mall

Location of trading area:
Suburban

Population:
- Primary trading area
  959,546
- Annualized percentage of shoppers
  anticipated to be from outside trade
  area: 35%

Development schedule:
- Opening date
  February 1964
- Renovation/expansion date
  October 6, 2006

Parking spaces:
- 6,400

*In renovating Westfield
Topanga in Canoga
Park, California,
designers reconfigured
the mall layout and
added new anchors.*

*I*n the Canoga Park suburb of Los Angeles, Westfield Topanga mall had a vacant anchor store space and sought to better serve its increasingly wealthy community with more upscale and luxurious stores. Adding Neiman Marcus as an anchor brought in the more upscale shopper. A new flagship Nordstrom is also part of the project.

The original covered 1960s mall had been cruciform in shape. The vacant Montgomery Ward store was cleared to create a racetrack layout, with Nordstrom and the Target anchoring the new corners. The racetrack also connects to existing Macy's and Sears stores. By reconfiguring the mall, the designers saw the opportunity to create distinct shopping districts, each appealing to a different type of shopper.

Regal architecture and striking structural elements mark the mall's center court. The shopping precincts took their names from

MAJOR TENANTS		
NAME	**TYPE**	**GLA (SQ. FT.)**
Macy's	Department store	251,000
Nordstrom	Department store	205,000
Sears	Department store	160,000
Target	Mass merchandiser	160,000
Neiman Marcus	Department store	120,000

Natural light (above) is balanced by theatrical lighting in other areas of the mall.

The Canyon district (right) contains river rocks and interior plantings.

nature: The Sky Garden, the Canyon, North Grove and the South Grove. The grove districts are defined by groups of palm trees. Existing structural elements are clad in limestone and walnut. Both grove precincts support two shopping levels: North Grove appealing to family, juniors and accessory shopping and South Grove serving as the housewares and home sector.

The Sky Garden rises 65 feet from ground to ceiling. Vertical retail and dramatic light define this section. Fashion images are projected

A diverse collection of restaurants is available to visitors of Westfield Topanga.

onto a two-story image wall, and a four-story skylit atrium reveals sky views beyond lush bamboo and connects retail to rooftop parking.

The Canyon is the heart of the project—a soaring space that evokes the outdoors with river rock and limestone paving, rock outcroppings, water features, trees and other landscaping. Two levels of luxury retail border the Canyon. The Dining Terrace is an extension of Canyon and offers upscale alfresco dining amidst umbrellas and trellises. The Quad, near the Target anchor store, offers family-friendly eateries, a

Photograph: Tom Bonner

double-decker carousel and the Westfield Playtown.

A new parking structure was the first itcm built in thc construction scheduling. By doing so, traffic was safely diverted to the area of the mall that would feel the least impact of the expansion and renovation. As other areas came to be active construction sites, they were cordoned off and segregated from the public. Most interior renovation was done after hours, reducing construction risk to the public. The developer also created an ongoing traffic-management plan that enabled construction workers to park off-site and ride shuttlcs to thc mall, leaving valuable parking spaces for holiday shoppers.

Other enhancements include concierge services, valet parking and theatrical lighting that provide simulated sunsets. The developer also committed to upgrade 20 intersections in the vicinity of the mall property, making sure the infrastructure would support the new shoppers finding their way to Westfield Topanga mall.

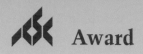

ATRIO

Villach, Austria

Owner and Development Company:
SES Spar European Shopping Centers
Salzburg, Austria

*I*n planning ATRIO as a tri-cultural shopping center near the intersection of Austria, Italy and Slovenia, the developers applied inventive techniques to manage energy, water, lighting, noise and air.

The center's in-situ concrete piles, which reach down over 160 feet, also serve as "energy piles"—the steady subterranean temperature allows water in the piles to be used in energy exchanges that heat and cool the center. In the summer, warmth created by cooling the building is passed into the ground rather than released into the atmosphere, both reducing costs and protecting the environment.

Water conservation techniques include a multi-story Alpen/Adriatic Water Column, which captures and recirculates water. Restroom basins use proximity sensors to conserve water. Surface water falling on the roofs is collected and seeps into the shopping center grounds rather than being passed on to the public wastewater network.

The center incorporates many other environmental enhance-ments. External lighting complies with European regulations that limit its impact on the night sky. Noise is reduced by placing parking lots on roofs and in underground garages. The building's facade serves as a thermal skin, helping to control temperature. Landscaping relies on limestone, gravel and natural tall grasses, rather than lawns. The architecture makes fullest use of renew-able resources. The building's overscaled glass skin includes glazing that offers both solar and ultraviolet protection.

ATRIO demonstrates that environmental protection can complement a high-quality shopping experience. For its pioneering approach and balanced realization, ATRIO wins this year's Award for Sustainable Design.

Photographs: © Thomas Jantscher

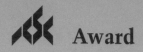

Westfield San Francisco Centre

San Francisco, California, United States

Owner and Development Company:
Forest City Enterprises/Westfield, LLC
Los Angeles, California, United States

Photograph: Courtesy of Westfield

By including the iconic Emporium department store in the renovation and expansion of Westfield San Francisco Centre, the project's developer and designers served both community pride and the needs of today's shoppers.

The Emporium, first built in 1896, is a celebration of Beaux-Arts classicism. Its facade survived the 1906 earthquake. The store was a shopping mecca throughout the 20th century, but closed in 1999. To merge the historic site into its planned expansion of the successful Westfield center, the developer spent nearly a half-billion dollars and engaged in almost a decade of planning and negotiation with city government.

Renovation logistics were extraordinary. The Emporium's famed 250-ton dome was raised 54 feet to top the renovated center, an effort acclaimed by engineering experts around the world. The dome's rotunda serves as a connection between the top floor of the Bloomingdale's anchor and the first floor of the Nordstrom

anchor, unifying the center despite San Francisco's topological variances. Escalators and stairwells incorporate original Art Deco balustrades, stairs and treads. The center's dual nature is shown in the Beaux-Arts architecture of one main entrance and the contemporary design of another. A city street was closed but through-block connections made the center appealing to pedestrians and riders of the subway and light rail lines.

The center now offers cutting-edge retail, entertainment, office and dining experiences. For its innovative concept and unparalleled execution, Westfield San Francisco Centre has earned the distinction as this year's Best of the Best.

Photograph: © Tim Griffith

Photograph: Courtesy of Westfield

Photograph: © Tim Griffith